BRICK
18

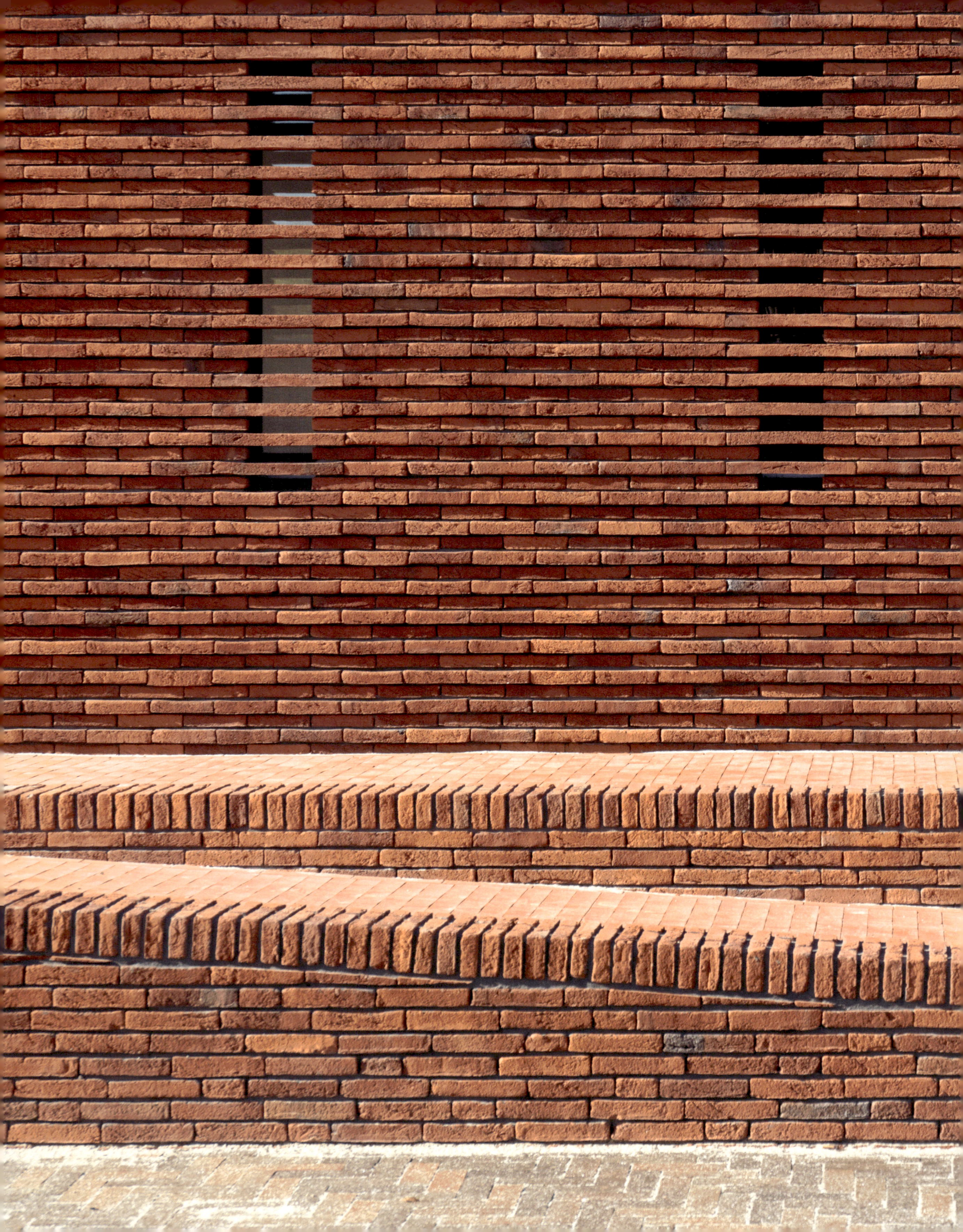

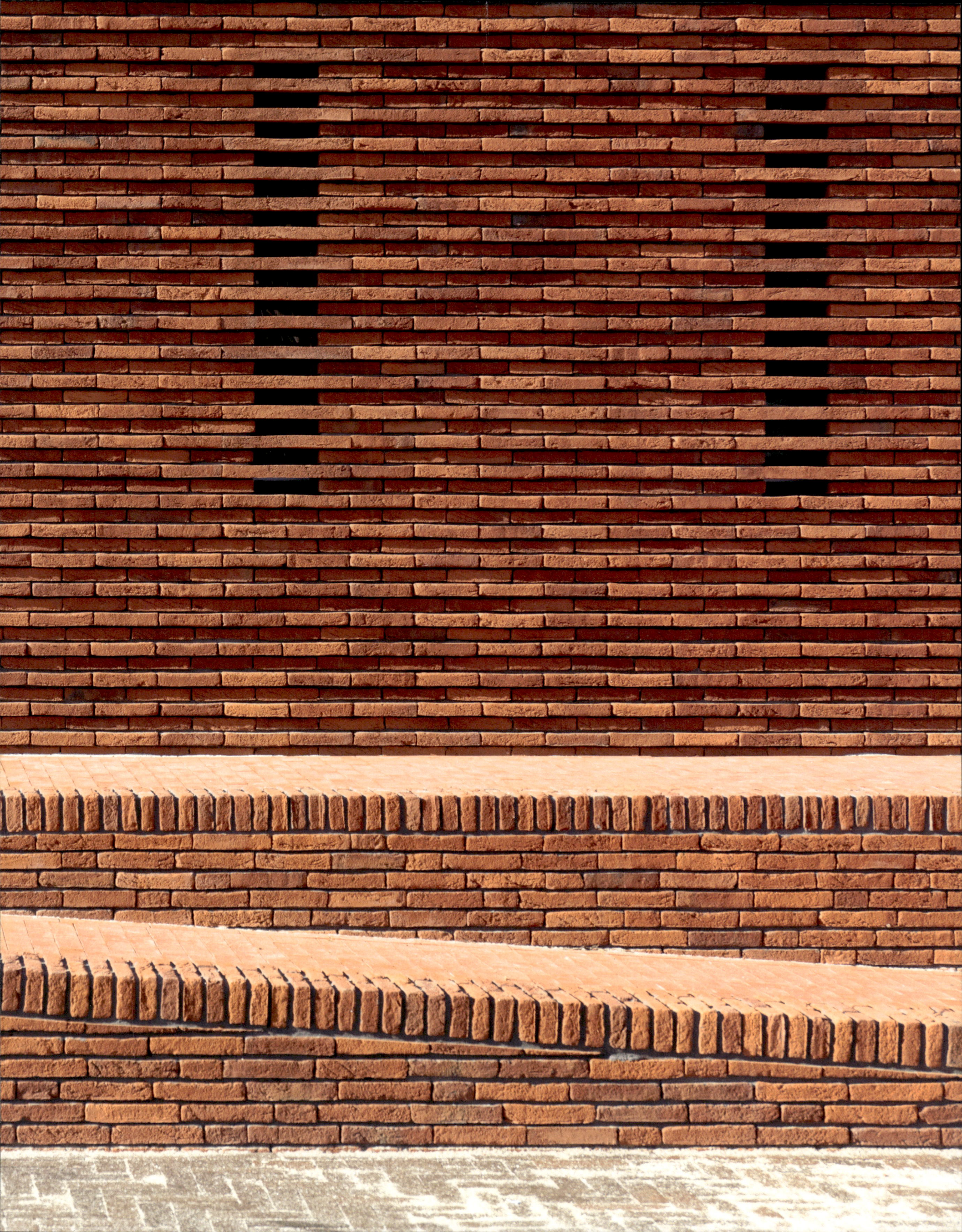

"The projects in the Brick Award show the very versatile ways brick is used as a contemporary form of construction and that brick architecture is widespread everywhere in the world." Jonathan Sergison

BRICK
18

PARK BOOKS

wienerberger

BRICK 18

Feeling at home

Living together

Working together

Sharing public spaces

Building outside the box

BRICK
18

Vladimir Arsene

Anne Kaestle

Jonathan Sergison, Marc Mimram and Anne Kaestle

Stephan Ferenczy

Jonathan Sergison

The Competition

The Brick Award provides architects from all over the world an opportunity to showcase modern, innovative architecture with bricks. It aims to inspire architects and people to share design concepts and explore new ways of fulfilling built ideas—made with ceramic materials.

2018 marks the eighth time that Wienerberger is presenting this internationally established award. Nearly 600 projects from 44 countries were submitted, this year with a particularly strong European focus. In the first phase of the two-part selection process, the 50 shortlisted projects were nominated by the pre-jury of international architects and architecture journalists from among the submissions. At every Brick Award, the composition and nationalities of this panel changes, and so do the sensitivities and tastes when assessing the projects. Wojciech Czaja, Christian Holl and Jan Peter Wingender, who also contributed project texts for this book, could be won over for the Brick Award 2018. As usual, the criteria for choosing the nominees and winners were the use of clay building materials, innovation, sustainability throughout the building process, and the architectural quality of the project. This year, however, the pre-jury members introduced a new, additional criterion which they called the "adequacy" of the project—"adequacy" meaning that it should also be regarded in relation to its purpose, building type and cultural context. A social project, for instance, is to be evaluated taking its limited budget into account.

When looking at this year's nominees, we can observe a number of tendencies that point toward current social and architecture trends. Many projects are located in an urban environment and these numerous renovation, extension and adaptation ventures reflect the growing demand for additional space within an urban context. It is also worth noting that the design of the buildings is often characterized by the forms and colors of facing and backing bricks and roof tiles: Abstract ornaments and structures are equally represented as lettering and structures that point to a historic context. Topics very present today across all industries—sustainability and user comfort—were likewise prominent. Several architects additionally adopted a playful approach to the architectural form, color or use of bricks, sometimes combined with other materials.

In the second phase, an international jury determined the winners of the competition. The architects Vladimir Arsene (Rumania), Stephan Ferenczy (Austria), Anne Kaestle (Switzerland), Marc Mimram (France) and Jonathan Sergison (Great Britain) met in Vienna to pick the winning projects from among the 50 nominees. The expertise and opinion of the jury were decisive, since Wienerberger had no say in the selection. Because the jury's enthusiasm for the projects was so high, they ultimately chose seven winners instead of five. During the judging procedure they particularly valued innovative architecture made with modest means, simple but smart concepts, as well as projects highlighting the versatility of clay building materials, e.g., for renovation purposes.

This book presents the 50 nominees, as well as the winners of the Brick Award 2018. Each project is also commented in a text written by one of the pre-jury members. Finally, the winners are featured in short videos you can find on brickaward.com.

Dear architecture fans, we wish you a lot of enjoyment in discovering the brick architecture masterpieces of the 2018 Brick Award!

"We believe in creating living spaces for human beings."
Heimo Scheuch
CEO Wienerberger

OUR MISSION

We improve people's quality of life by providing outstanding, sustainable building material and infrastructure solutions.

Editorial

Dear Friends of Architecture,

In this 21st century, we are experiencing an era of global challenges: climate change, a growing world population, demographic aging and massive migration movements. Add to these the accelerating trend of urbanization, changing mobility patterns and the transformation of the world of work, as well as progressive digitalization and the resultant blurring of geographic borders. All these developments have a direct bearing on people's lifestyle choices and, thus, also on the kind of buildings they want to inhabit—today and in the future. In urban areas, particularly, this calls for innovative approaches that address and reflect these developments by creating attractive residential and work environments.

In this context, architecture assumes a mediating role by configuring the connections between people and the built environment. It addresses the challenges of today and tomorrow by working with new shapes, materials and concepts of use. Apart from aesthetic aspirations, there are stringent technical regulations and increasingly demanding quality requirements to be met. Sustainability issues, such as energy-efficient building and recyclability, are as imperative as they are self-evident these days. At the same time, the affordability of housing is an essential aspect to be borne in mind.

Today, building projects are no longer the sum total of individual materials or the product of isolated trades, but the result of holistic concepts. Intelligent digital design and tailor-made system solutions are of prime importance, as are innovative, smart and interconnected building materials. Choosing the best-suited building elements is essential. Bricks, for example, can be used for a broad range of applications, given their characteristics and their variability in terms of design. As natural and sustainable building materials that are technologically sophisticated and innovative, bricks remain as attractive as ever today.

However, regardless of how much progress we have made in terms of technology, the most important point of reference in architecture is still the individual. When creating new living space, the prime focus will always be on human beings and their needs.

On the occasion of the eighth Wienerberger Brick Award, we proudly recognize the high quality of the brick architecture projects submitted from all over the world. Our thanks are due to the jury of experts and their valuable contribution to the selection process, as well as to all the architects involved: With your future-oriented concepts, you are creating innovative living spaces. You are meeting the architectural challenges of the 21st century with new ideas and the courage to explore new avenues. I hope that all friends of architecture will enjoy reading the BRICK Book 2018 and derive inspiration from the discovery of these extraordinary architecture.

Heimo Scheuch

Feeling at home

Living together

Working together

Sharing public spaces

Building outside the box

Feeling at home

WOLFGANG PAUSER

Why Do Bricks Warm the Soul? – Emotional and Cultural Connotations of Mock Stones

Wolfgang Pauser

In order to promote expressionist glass architecture, in 1919 architect Adolf Behne argued polemically with expressive and crude words against traditional "stone architecture." The worst accusation he made against masonry buildings involved their "nebulous, extreme homeliness" and the "drunken card players in the corner" who live in them. Transparent glass buildings would rehabilitate them into modern people with "clarity of consciousness" and a completely rational way of life. The bright light would act "like a crack of the whip."

Fortunately, this utopia never came to pass. What remains is the emotional bond between bricks and the human soul. Today we would never even think of vilifying the comfort and coziness of brick architecture. Rather, we seek physical as well as psychological warmth in the ruddy bricks. The question is, how and why this building material succeeds in arousing warm feelings of familiarity and cozy comfort.

Trust is a feeling that establishes a bond. It grows over time. The brick satisfies the need for familiarity in two ways. Firstly, through the millennia that have passed since its invention, which have burned themselves into our cultural memory and, to this day, continue to shape myths, traditions and symbols in, as it were, an archetypal way. The brick, our mock stone, is so old that it is indeed customarily perceived as something entirely natural. Secondly, through the durability of the material – which becomes plainly evident on those ancient buildings whose bricks are laid bare. That is why the word 'brick' is still primarily associated with the historical clay brick – the solid brick that you can hold in one hand, which is used both as cladding and structure, although the reality of modern brick construction is determined by myriad shapes and materials for a wide range of requirements and applications, from floors to the roof.

The archetypal brick differs from its present physical reality, and attempts are often made to bridge this difference by creating a façade of facing bricks that are affixed to an exterior wall constructed of modern walling blocks, thus using decoration to present the inner substance to the outside world. Among the many cases in which reality and appearance diverge from each other, this type of construction is so special because the veneer wants not to deceive but to tell the truth. Evidently, the block is an element whose true being needs a veneer. Its emotional dimension emerges most clearly where its functional substance and its physical appearance are split apart. What predestines the typical brick to attract desire and emotion?

> "The brick satisfies the need for familiarity."

The traditional brick is tangible in two senses: the physical and the notional. Its dimensions are tailored for the hand: it is just light and small enough to be gripped in one hand and passed on along a human chain. Its "human dimension" also applies to its being grasped in the cognitive sense. Like the natural crystal, the man-made brick is a geometric object. It embodies the human cognitive tool of geometry and thus makes it halfway to being understood. We can blindly trust its uniformity. That makes it the prototype of all abstract entities with which the human mind "builds" its models, from the basics of mathematics to the planetary system. Scientific thought has difficulties disengaging from building metaphors; it constantly needs objects and elements like atoms, genes, bits, and bytes in order to imagine reality as assembled and "built up." Even book titles like "Building Blocks of a Theory of Religious Understanding" are common. And although the epochal invention of modularity is a forerunner of today's digital world view, the simplicity and complete tangibility of the brick have the emotional function of promising us symbolic salvation from the overcomplexity and growing incomprehensibility of the world. Its elemental nature sustains our trust in the world.

Not only its form, but also its relationship to the material strengthens our feeling of trust in the brick. The inherent inner homogeneity of the building material makes the brick's visible surface into a symbol of its depth. As opposed to an exterior that is coated or painted, the surface of the brick conveys the illusion of being able, as it were, to look into its dark interior and also to fully represent its substance in its appearance. The concept of "authenticity," which originates from the aesthetics of functionalist modernism, ennobles the brick with categories of knowledge, communication, and a morality of honesty. As conceptual opposition to lies that arouse mistrust, the brick emerges as a symbol of intrinsic veracity, as something authentic that mobilizes feelings of trust even where it is used as a veneer. Brick façades effortlessly deflect the enlightened general suspicion of all appearances – the belief that one must "always look behind the façade" to get to the bottom of the "truth."

> "The traditional brick is tangible in two senses: the physical and the notional."

Along with its form and material, the brick's traditional means of production is also a source of mythological connotations. German words such as "Backstein" and "Ziegelbäcker" (literally "baked stone" and "brick baker") can be traced back to shared preindustrial technology. In the fairy tale "Hansel and Gretel," the walls and roof tiles of the witch's house are made of gingerbread to lure the forsaken children inside. In both German and English vernacular, "a bun in the oven" is a metaphor for pregnancy. Symbolically loaded with motherliness and cake baking, every brick house is suffused with a pinch of gingerbread fragrance for the soul.

MONADNOCK

Atlas House

Job Floris and Sandor Naus

PROJECT NAME
Atlas House

ARCHITECT/S
Monadnock, Rotterdam / NL

BUILDING PURPOSE
Single-family housing

LOCATION
Eindhoven, The Netherlands

CONSTRUCTION PERIOD
2015–2016

BRICK TYPE
Facing bricks

BRICK AWARD CATEGORY
Feeling at home

BRICK 18 Category Winner

Situated on the edge of a typical suburban development in Eindhoven along a large green estate, this house with a garden blends at first sight into its surroundings. It meets the local building code that orders for white, cubic houses to be situated between the existing trees. However, on closer inspection the house reveals a refined play of mass and material that challenges all conventions.

Positioned at a 45-degree angle on the plot, it rises in a single gesture to the maximum allowed building height, lending the house a tower-like appearance. The subtle curved roof ending provokes the building mass resonating with the image of historical watchtowers. Strangely enough, the curve suggests the absence of an even larger spherical volume that used to be the top of the house. A load being taken off, leaving this sturdy figure behind in its new surroundings. Hence its name: Atlas House.

The house is constructed in red bricks with rough, outpouring joints that enhance its archetypical and robust character. The bi-colored façade provides it with a plinth and a lighter top, while leaving the red bricks visible in the reveals of the windows. To indicate the entrance, the white cement render is used as a minimal embellishment recalling the Dutch Renaissance traditions.

> "The footprint of the house is minimized within the given building height, resulting in a vertically organized program."

The window openings are grouped around the corners, allowing for diagonal views through the house. When entering the house, the red bricks continue on the inside as bare ceramic building blocks of the same size as the façade, effectively suggesting the monolithic character of the wall. Since the finish of the house is minimal, it leaves the standard building products from which the house is constructed visible. The ongoing middle wall divides it into a "serving" area around the wooden built-in stair and a "served" side that consists of the three floors with rooms of different proportions. In the middle wall the ceramic blocks are put on their side, thus revealing a smooth surface that contrasts with the standard rough texture of the bricks.

Built in the simplest construction materials, the Atlas House displays a perfect control over the application of materials. By leaving all materials and fixtures exposed, great effort is put in the execution. Mistakes, therefore, cannot be "covered up" afterwards. The precise proportioning, the placement of the windows at the corners and the exposed materials lend each room an intense, highly articulated character. Oscillating between the comfort of an introverted castle room and the nakedness of rough construction, the Atlas House is to be conquered by its inhabitants.

The Atlas House is an overwhelming play with references, traditions and suggestions. The suggested simplicity of the house is misleading. Material and execution are carefully considered, taking the maximum out of each component. The brickworks both in- and outside are carefully detailed and are constitutional to the house. Moreover, the deliberate choice of modest material and minimal finishes lends the house a radicalism that can be found in some works of art. And yet the Atlas House remains a house; domestic and surprisingly comfortable and by doing so, it challenges all conventions of suburban domestic architecture.

The roof could have carried a large sphere—that's why it is called the "Atlas House."

The positioning of the windows allows a diagonal vista from the inside and outside.

Jury Statement

"A private living space organized on three floors on a small plot. Not a house located in a tremendously exciting way on a lakeside or with a beautiful view to a mountain panorama, and also not part of the mainstream. It is a very normal house and has its own qualities. We think it is a good answer to what kind of quality housing can be built with—of how private, small-scale housing can look in the future. The strength of the project is related to the material of brick because it is used on the inside and outside consistently. You find the same material in different colors for different room atmospheres. It is very strictly a brick house outside and inside."

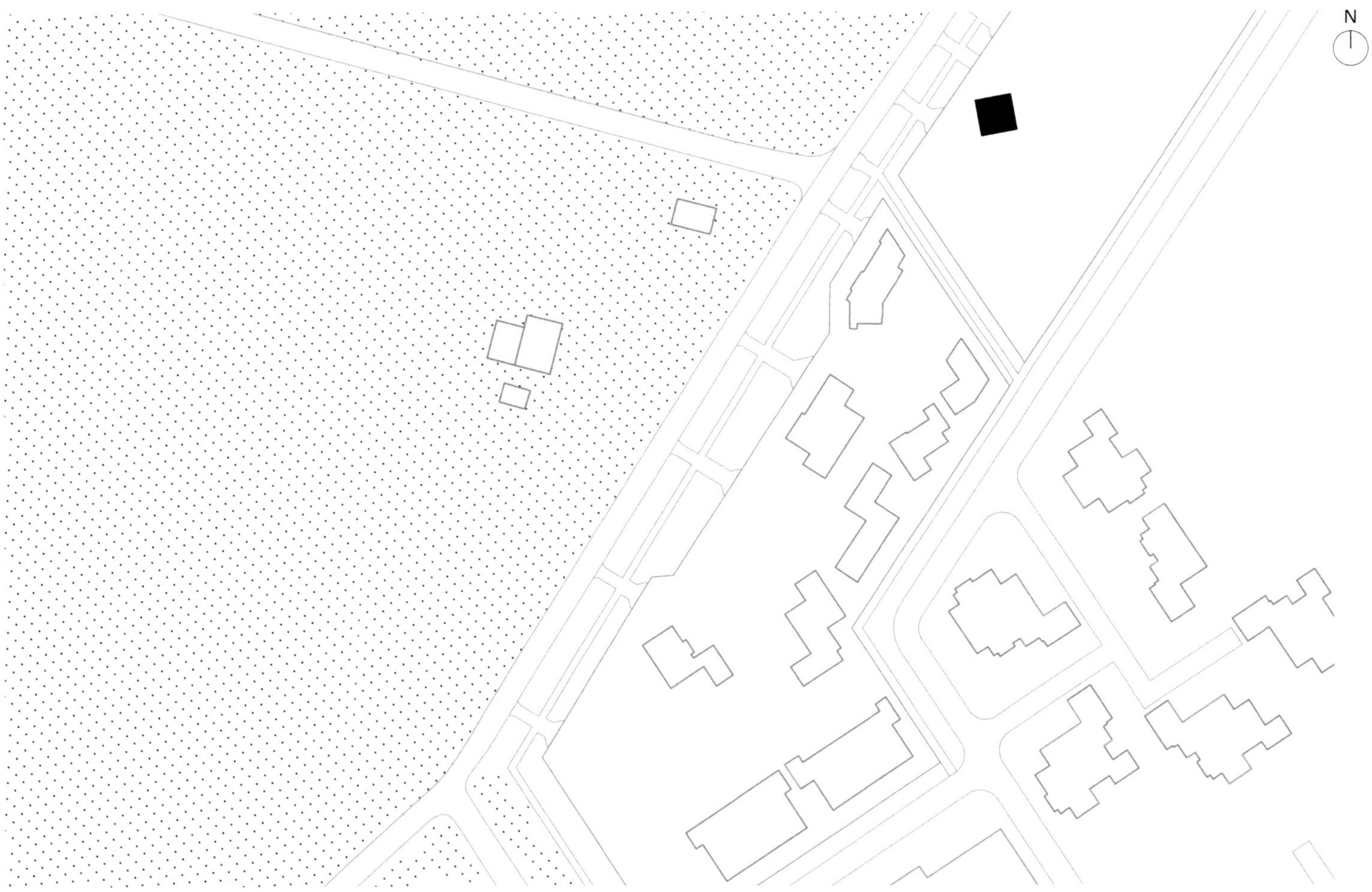

Site plan

The south side of the house with the entrance

Red bricks are also found in the window reveals.

The mixture of red and white bricks provides for a strong, graphic impression.

Brick is the defining material in the house's interior as well.

Views from the south, north, west and east from bottom left in a clockwise direction

Villa Platan

Martin Laursen, Martin Krogh and Anders Lonka

PROJECT NAME
Villa Platan

ARCHITECT/S
ADEPT,
Copenhagen / DK

BUILDING PURPOSE
Single-family housing

LOCATION
Aarhus, Denmark

CONSTRUCTION PERIOD
2012–2015

BRICK TYPE
Clay blocks

BRICK AWARD CATEGORY
Feeling at home

In Hans Christian Andersen's most famous fairytale, "The Little Mermaid" dreams of leaving the water one day and exploring the coast. "Now the oldest princess was fifteen years old and was to venture above the surface," the Danish storyteller wrote in the year 1837. "When she came back, she had hundreds of things to tell, but the most delightful, she said, was to lie in the moonlight on a sandbank in the calm water, and to see close to the coast the great city, where the lights twinkled like hundreds of stars." At Villa Platan, not far from Aarhus, one has to inevitably think about the story of the young nixie.

"Nothing shall disturb the dialog with nature."

As if the house had always been here—the villa actually has more of a lying mermaid to it than a standing structure, soaring upwards—, it blends with nature at the point where land and water come together. Color, shape and size do not disturb the shoreline in any way whatsoever. "We carefully designed the building and in the process concentrated on the colors occurring here," the architect Anders Lonka points out. "It is as if the daily changes between sky and water would become a part of the architecture, a part of the DNA of this house."

Towards the street, the Villa Platan appears serene and closed, yet the ground floor bungalow opens toward the sea with large, floor-to-ceiling glazing. Sand, reed, stones and trees encroach into the interior like three-dimensional images. Nearly invisible, the outer walls meld into this potpourri of reduced, desaturated colors. The façade consists of oblong, very flat, sand-colored bricks.

Bleached timber planks and custom-made, solid-oak furniture in the interior consort with the mineral material on the façade. "Nothing shall disturb the dialog with nature," says the architect. "It's about the fantastic view and a beautiful, simple life in flux." This also explains the amorphous layout of the structure, which is made of four cubes that flow together at the corners into a spatial continuum between inside and outside in an apparently coincidental manner. The rounded room edges create exciting long views between the foyer, kitchen, living room and bedroom. One reaches the partially cellared area of the house, where a TV room and two small guest rooms are located, via stairs. The rest is the endless ocean.

How does it go in Hans Christian Andersen's tale? "Down by the coast there were lovely green forests [...]. The shore formed a small bay here where the water was completely still but very deep, all the way to the cliff where fine silver sand had been washed up."

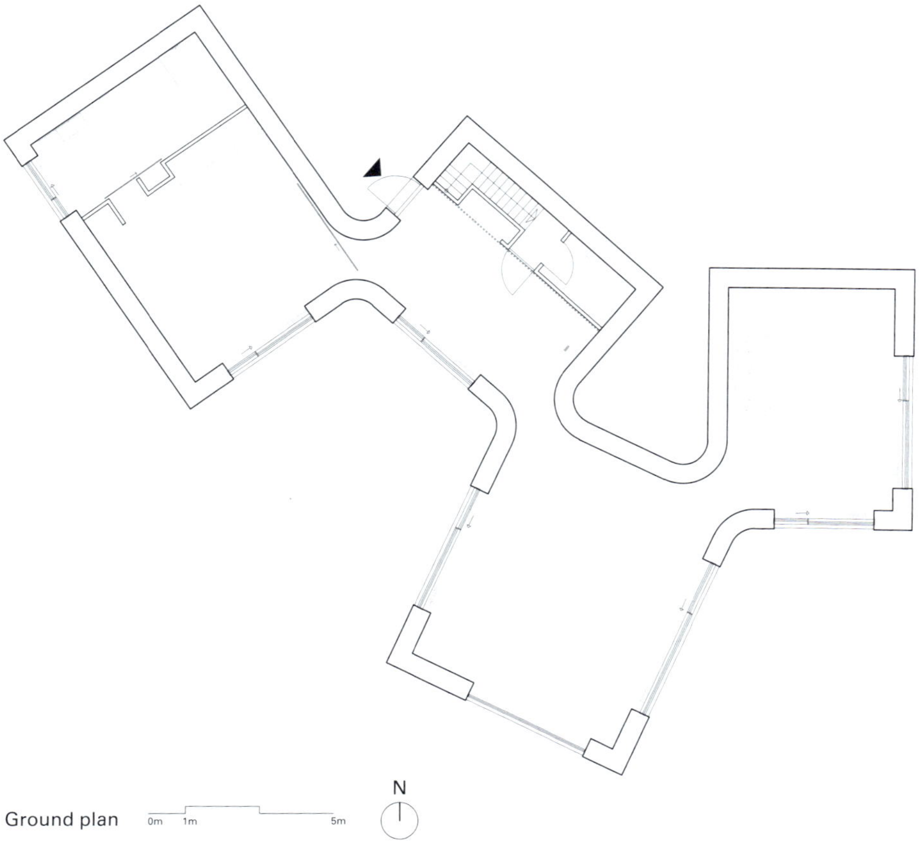

Ground plan

A protected courtyard opens towards the southwest.

The materialization is oriented to the colors of the surroundings.

View from the beach

SWAN ARCHITECTES

Social Housing in the Vines & Public Garden

Joachim Bellemin, Serge Rodrigues and Ambroise Bera

PROJECT NAME
Social Housing in the Vines & Public Garden

ARCHITECT/S
Swan Architectes, Paris / FR

BUILDING PURPOSE
Social housing

LOCATION
Bouzy, France

CONSTRUCTION PERIOD
2014–2015

BRICK TYPE
Facing bricks

BRICK AWARD CATEGORY
Feeling at home

The best and most famous sparkling wines in the world come from the Champagne region. Colorful labels from the houses of Pommery, Veuve Clicquot and Piper-Heidsieck are familiar to every sommelier and wine connoisseur. In Bouzy, just 20 kilometers south of the historic commercial city of Reims, a Paris-based architect's office followed the example of this tradition and decorated its houses with pastel-colored labels in the form of window shutters, metal railings and small tool sheds that were boldly placed into the landscape.

"Does social housing always have to look like social housing," the architect asks. One of the core competences of the studio is the concentration on sustainability and durability, as well as the sometimes surprising combination of noble, high-quality construction materials and inexpensive, industrial, mass-produced goods. The dialog of the extremes has already yielded many a radical, distinctive structure—an impish wink not excluded. "With this project as well, we decided to reinterpret the game rules of social housing construction and gave our quartet a traditional handwriting that is connected with the local building technique, but is also individual."

The construction consists of brightly-fired facing bricks. Sand-colored with a slight pink tinge, the tone seems directly extracted from the soil around here. Furthermore, the seemingly archaic construction method is oriented to the vineyards and the industrial buildings of Champagne Province. Brick masonry, zinc roofing and the classic pitched roof have had a long tradition in this branch and region. At first sight, it seems as if one would not see hardly anything private, anything homey in this building ensemble in the middle of the vines—if it wasn't for the cheerful, coquettish accents and accessories in sky blue, spring green, lavender and sunflower yellow.

"Our desire? To give the notion of social housing a makeover, through houses that dialog with the surrounding residential area, while redefining the aesthetics of the genre."

Concealed behind the asymmetrical façades with their irregularly sloping ridges are four single-family houses with four rooms each on two floors and 95 square meters of living space, which were erected for the municipal property developer Châlons-en-Champagne Habitat. There is a good reason for the compact design: In this way, a part of the area could remain undeveloped and is now a small, publicly accessible park for the populace of Bouzy. The aesthetic of small shrubs, as the architects call it, enters into a dialog with the surrounding vineyards. Certainly, Mother Nature still needs some time before she unfolds her entire splendor, but one already gets a sparkling notion that a small piece of luxury has arisen here for everyone.

Design model

A public park developed together with the housing estate.

Window and door shutters place colorful accents in the quiet brick façades.

PEDEVILLA ARCHITECTS

House on Mühlbach

Armin and Alexander Pedevilla

PROJECT NAME
House on Mühlbach

ARCHITECT/S
Pedevilla Architects, Bruneck / IT

BUILDING PURPOSE
Single-family housing

LOCATION
Sand in Taufers, Italy

CONSTRUCTION PERIOD
2012–2014

BRICK TYPE
Clay blocks

BRICK AWARD CATEGORY
Feeling at home

Mountains soar into the sky in the background and it almost seems as if the small, single-family house in Sand in Taufers would try to trace the rugged, irregular contour of the Alpine peaks. From some vantage points the white monolith fits harmonically into the natural surroundings; from others, however, it has the effect of a lonely castle keep or one of those manor houses proudly placed into the landscape, which are so common in South Tyrol. Especially dramatic is the perspective seen from the whooshing Mühlbach stream, which nestles around the house like a chillingly cold passe-partout.

> "Location and history must always bear a relation to each other. This also means that we indeed create modern, contemporary architecture, but this is always based on the traditional art of building and classical craftsmanship."

"We place importance on the fact that our architecture establishes a connection between today and the world of yesterday," says Armin Pedevilla, who runs the Pedevilla Architects office together with his brother Alexander. "Location and history must always bear a relation to each other. This also means that we indeed create modern, contemporary architecture, but this is always based on the traditional art of building and classical craftsmanship." The so-called "House on Mühlbach" melds these apparent opposites into a perfect, precisely designed composition.

A solidly bricked pentagon that pulls itself over a total of seven split levels up under the roof constitutes the basic shape. 50-centimeter-thick bricks were used to do this. On the outside, the solid brick structure is draped in a coarse plaster dress made of lime, white cement and local sands, lending the house a unique mixture of rough dullness and glittering precision. "South Tyrol is a very tradition-conscious region," Pedevilla points out, "and we try to respect that. From our long-term experience we know that manually-applied, mineral plasters blend well with the townscape and landscape, and are also well-accepted by the local population."

The façade is structured by variously sized, square window openings, which are freely distributed across the large wall surfaces. The location and size of the windows were carefully geared to the space utilization, the furnishings and the view. Details in opaquely waxed bronze and coarsely scraped elmwood for the entrance door set elegant accents. Topping everything off are rhombus-shaped roof tiles made by hand from white cement and dolomite sand and then sand-blasted.

> "We place importance on the fact that our architecture establishes a connection between today and the world of yesterday."

Artisanal precision work characterizes the interiors as well. The elaborately mixed, filled and smoothed out plaster consists of slaked lime, marble sands and earth pigments from the immediate surroundings. Passeir gneiss, as well as doors, flooring and built-in furniture made of hand-planed elmwood have also been added. Along the centrally located wooden stairs, the open single space twists itself up to below the roof, forming several open living and sleeping galleries in this way. The material and topographic subtlety is found in the detail.

The topography of the landscape and the house

Precisely orchestrated views

The brick masonry was rendered with a plaster made of lime, white cement and local sands.

BLOCK ARCHITECTS

Lee&Tee House

Dang Duc Hoa

PROJECT NAME
Lee&Tee House

ARCHITECT/S
Block Architects,
Ho Chi Minh City / VN

BUILDING PURPOSE
Single-family housing / office

LOCATION
Ho Chi Minh City, Vietnam

CONSTRUCTION PERIOD
2016

BRICK TYPE
Facing bricks

BRICK AWARD CATEGORY
Feeling at home

The gap site is precisely four meters wide. In the lively northern part of the commercial metropolis of Ho Chi Minh City, a classic craftsman's house once stood here on a 72-square-meter area. The spaces were narrow and dark. At the request of the client, the house was to be rebuilt. Block Architects decided to demolish large parts of the building and to reduce the structure to the constructive minimum. Only the delineating brick walls left and right along the property border remained.

"We removed everything unnecessary in order to get light and air inside again," the architects point out. "And although both firewalls seem slender and unimposing, they are capable of bearing the load of the entire house." Instead of solid outer walls there are large-area glass façades; in place of the old wooden ceilings there are now, like in a house of cards so to speak, weightless, horizontal cement slabs stretched between the two brick walls. Where banisters, wall paneling and bulky cement stairs earlier were, there is now an ultra-thin replacement in the form of white-lacquered structural steel.

"Usually," the architects say, "these rebars are used to fortify reinforced concrete constructions. We took advantage of their high firmness and used them as a three-dimensional, geometric matrix." The white lattice serves as a stair landing, fall protection, bookshelf, bench on the terrace, as well as a trellis for all kinds of creepers. And repeatedly peeking through here and there—following the own rules of the grid—is the old brick structure still able to bear the load.

"It's almost as if the architects sewed this house together just like the way we also stitch our bags. Many fine, white threads are spun between both leather walls and ultimately give it its shape."

The living area resembles an urban jungle. Ferns, bushes and trees thrive next to the kitchenette on the ground floor. In the background the flora spreads upwards on a vertical, green wall. Sleeping areas for the parents and the children, as well as an attic floor with quiet areas and a separate roof terrace, hover above. It is a surreal life inside and outside, between old bricks and an airy void.

"This house means everything to us," the residents explain, "since we are now able to reap the fruit of our labor after years of effort." The young married couple, who lives here together with their two children, works in the clothing industry and produces handcrafted leather bags and accessories. "It's almost as if the architects sewed this house together just like the way we also stitch our bags. Many fine, white threads are spun between both leather walls and ultimately give it its shape."

The Lee&Tee House is not only a radical living and life concept, but also an extraordinary example of the respectful and resource-saving dealing with a robust, long-lasting building material that can be staged in many ways.

Steel rebars serve, among other things, as trellises.

The surface of the brick walls underscores the spatial oscillation between the inside and outside.

Both firewalls carry the load of the entire building.

RUSSELL JONES

Mews House

Russell Jones

PROJECT NAME
Mews House

ARCHITECT/S
Russell Jones,
London / GB

BUILDING PURPOSE
Single-family housing

LOCATION
London, Great Britain

CONSTRUCTION PERIOD
2014–2015

BRICK TYPE
Facing bricks

BRICK AWARD CATEGORY
Feeling at home

Mews are originally buildings used as stables on the back side of London residential houses. Later they served as workshops or storage spaces before houses were frequently built in their place. In this case as well, the Mews House in the London district of Highgate, a disused garage and a derelict garden were replaced by a house—one that stands out on account of a careful choice and handling of materials, as well as through a clear spatial concept and, because of that, radiates an unpretentious, elegant atmosphere in spite of the cramped conditions. The site only measures 90 square meters; the house emerging upon it has about 70 square meters of floor space to offer. Skilful designing was demanded, since every spatial disturbance created here leads to a feeling of narrowness. Minimalism is, in this case, not an attitude, but a necessity.

"The project was designed and developed with an economy of visual, spatial and structural means. The material palette and the design were kept intentionally simple."

On the unpartitioned ground floor one finds the living space with a kitchen unit, which opens up to a small courtyard. Two small rooms with space-saving, built-in furniture and a bathroom are located on the top floor. The architect selected materials that take the context into account, but accentuate the new building nevertheless with an individual touch. With wood for the stairs, the window frames, the floorboards on the upper story and the white surfaces of the built-in furniture and doors, an atmosphere was created, which, in its directness and simplicity, corresponds to the house, its size, the location and its history, and lets one think of a small loft. But a special role is particularly played by the bricks chosen for the inner and outer walls. A yellowish brick with a varying, seemingly handcrafted surface was coated with white-gray slurry, so that the house appears very bright, but the single bricks are still recognized well. The treatment of the brick with burlap or with a brush is based on a traditional process from Scandinavia. Originally from Australia, the architect had gotten to know and appreciate this technique in Denmark, where he lived for a long time. Small niches for candles, plants or other objects are incorporated into the brickwork wall in the courtyard.

"The quality of the brickwork has been enhanced through the use of a carefully selected mortar and a subtle manipulation of the surface texture using a method known in Scandinavia as 'Sækkeskuring'."

Due to the tight location—the front houses are four stories high after all—and the single-sided orientation, additional sources of light were tapped with the small courtyard and skylights, the effect of which is improved by the bright surfaces. Whether the entrance front with side glazing, the story-high opening to the inner courtyard, the bright wood and the floorboards on the ground floor that merge from the exterior to the interior and were chosen in a shade corresponding to the walls, or whether the louver, which brings indirect light into the stairwell and widens the space upwards: the architect also proved in the details to be a master in accomplishing the best result in a confined space.

The new house integrates into the row of the existing mews in a completely self-evident way.

Niches are incorporated into the brick walls of the inner courtyard as ornamental shelf spaces.

The bright brick intensifies the effect of the indirect daylight.

Brick, wood, glass and concrete encounter each other here in a subtle way.

HERMANSSON HILLER LUNDBERG ARKITEKTER

House Juniskär

Andreas Hermansson, Andreas Hiller and Samuel Lundberg

PROJECT NAME
House Juniskär

ARCHITECT/S
Hermansson Hiller Lundberg Arkitekter, Stockholm / SE

BUILDING PURPOSE
Single-family housing

LOCATION
Sundsvall, Sweden

CONSTRUCTION PERIOD
2013–2015

BRICK TYPE
Facing bricks

BRICK AWARD CATEGORY
Feeling at home

A "reflection on the theme of the domestic" is how the architects of the house in the Swedish coastal town of Sundsvall describe it. Situated on a flat slope with a view to the water, the property is used by the architects to combine the outwardly simple-appearing composition of two structures joined together with an interior offering many variants. A shorter, two-story volume is set to the side of an elongated, single-story one. Both are topped with a slightly pitched roof.

"The uniform and ornamental treatment of the brick surface is underlined by the precise placement of the windows in relation to the bricklaying logic, which also gives the house a classic and monolithic appearance."

The lower building takes up the garage in the front part; a wooden-clad, cut-in area serves as the house entrance. A staircase leads left from the entrance hallway half a floor above to the bathroom and bedroom; straight ahead, stairs that become increasingly wider downwards open to the high and spacious living area. Here the spatial concept of the house, which is indebted to the "Raumplan" idea of Adolf Loos, becomes clear. This idea assumes that variously used spaces ought to have a different height in order to attain comfortable and pleasant proportions. With this three-dimensional thinking not only are surfaces added, but constructive bodies are melded into a composition. The position on the slope promotes this here in an ideal manner: The flatter volume can develop as a higher space towards the water while the second structure can absorb the lower sleeping area, as well as the kitchen underneath, which likewise opens towards the garden and the water. It is not divided from the living room by a wall; the change in the flooring, however, from wood parquet to dark red tile, marks the border between the two realms. In this way, the elegant proportions become tangible, since the hallway, stairs, living space and kitchen are not separated from each other by doors. Kept in various hues and framed in white, the walls lend the small house a dignified atmosphere.

On the exterior, too, the appreciation of the interior proportions is reflected. The larger structure is lower, the smaller one higher—the exterior appearance is thus also staged in a balanced fashion. The spatial composition is accentuated by the uniform brick façade over a flat concrete base. It consists of Danish bricks laid in an English cross bond; the windowsills are also made of brick. The color of the brick varies from russet to dark brown. Despite the uniformity, a lively surface is thereby created; thanks to it, the house blends harmonically into the nature of the surroundings. The sizes of the window openings and the color of the window frames, as well as the roofing, are likewise sensitively matched with the façade. Out of a supposedly simple task and a common repertoire, an unobtrusive, yet noble house developed, one which made a principle quality out of its simplicity.

"The house has a sort of doubleness, or Janus-character, since it is formal and symmetrical towards the garden but informal and plastic towards the entrance side."

View from the living area with high room heights going outwards.

The color and structure of the brick façades are restrained and lively at the same time.

The garage is on the front left; the incised entrance is on the side.

The window reveals are also clad with brick.

PROJECT ORANGE

Foundry Mews

Christopher Ash and James Soane

PROJECT NAME
Foundry Mews

ARCHITECT/S
Project Orange, London / GB

BUILDING PURPOSE
Single-family housing / studio workspaces

LOCATION
London, Great Britain

CONSTRUCTION PERIOD
2014–2016

BRICK TYPE
Facing bricks
Paving bricks

BRICK AWARD CATEGORY
Feeling at home

Just off the River Thames in West London, Barnes High Street is a typical street where shops, amenities and small businesses have lined up throughout the years. With only their small fronts facing the street, many of the businesses and workshops spread into the deep backside within the building block. On the site of a former car body repair workshop, Project Orange created a combined living and working environment employing the traditional model of a mew.

> "Foundry Mews makes sustainable use of a previously light industrial brownfield site, decontaminating the land and allowing an abandoned urban site a new lease of life."

Through a passage from the street one enters the winding mew with eight ateliers and workshop spaces along it. Two open stairs give direct access to the six maisonettes that are situated above. Although there is a clear horizontal division between the workshop and the maisonettes on top, the ensemble reads as a row of small houses with pitched roofs that reflects the scale of the space and the surrounding buildings. The mew is closed in the back by slightly bigger houses accommodating two offices or studio spaces and an apartment on top. Building on the plot was difficult, since all materials had to be transported by hand from the street through the small passage. The plinth was constructed in concrete, the houses above in a blockwork and timber construction with a limited, yet refined interior finish leaving constructive elements visible. The façades of the houses are constructed in a soft yellow/gray brick. The brick façades adapt to the surroundings and make a clear reference to the industrial past of the site. The flooring of the mew and the stairs are covered in a paver that fits very well to the bricks. Together with the cladding of the lower part of the division wall along the mew, the light colors create both a uniformity and intimacy determining the character of the ensemble.

> "The client's long-term vision has facilitated a sustainable community that is robust and resilient."

The brickwork façades are finished with flush mortar joints and the window openings are carefully detailed into the brickwork. On the upper floor the private terraces of the houses are screened off with a perforated brick wall and the façades are finished with a band of projecting bricks, adding texture to them and balancing the composition of the whole ensemble. The programmatic mix and density of the scheme is well resolved through the careful organization of private outdoor spaces of the houses and the harmonic organization of the mews and the stairs. The use of a single material provides unity and scale to the ensemble that showcases a desirable way of living and working in our contemporary cities.

Longitudinal section

Site plan

Bricks rotating out of the façade at a 90-degree angle structure the surfaces.

A perforated brick wall affords privacy on the upper floor.

Living together

MARCOS PARGA / ESTUDIO MAPAA

The RRURBAN Effect

Marcos Parga

I want to tell you the story of how a design commission became the unexpected starting point for an intense and open-ended investigation. A few months ago we received a call from a private developer, asking for ideas to build a small residential block, set in a plot between buildings in the center of Madrid. For several reasons, we decided to deploy a solution that could be easily adapted to any infill site in the center of our cities, thus increasing the possibilities for the project to come true.

The first question we asked ourselves was crucial: What type of home do we deserve?

Many urbanites would think that the new residential architectures shall give us the possibility to live in the city with all its density and effervescence, while enjoying some of the advantages of the (idealized) rural environment. However, our everyday reality shows us the opposite, and that's why we decided to open up our design process to indeterminacy and participation. The goal was to develop a protocol of action with the aim of replacing the unifying trend of urbanization by operations that exploit diversity and contact with nature.

The RRURBAN strategy (Really RURAL and URBAN) is based on some of the conclusions of a research process that aims to reflect on a new way of understanding community life in our cities through architecture. The strategy can be seen as a possible way to introduce the benefits of single-family housing in the speculative DNA of collective housing, activating, moreover, issues related to participatory design. We soon came to the conclusion that to achieve that kind of hybrid, our strategy should combine two actions on the urban housing typology: hollow out and customize. The former to generate spaces of opportunity for the final users (non-predefined use), and the latter to be able to increase the value of each house and thus economically compensate the decrease of built area. From this point, everything was easier: We must only substitute the unifying tendency of urban construction with operations that exploit diversity. We would then come back to a certain degree of personalization that in turn creates identity and redefines our way of living together. Besides, this path allows us to explore the limits of participation, as already done by John Habraken with his theories about the "open-building" or Frei Otto with his „Ökohaus" ("Eco House") many years ago. Habraken, in his crucial book *Supports: An Alternative to Mass Housing* (1972) stated as a premonition: "Even within the same income group there are many families and individuals with widely differing backgrounds, ambitions, and living habits. How can mass housing deal with that? [...] it means ... that before we can introduce the natural relationship, we must find a way to build independent dwellings on top of each other."
Supports advocated for an approach where the technicians – architects, engineers and construction companies – working with the state provided the infrastructure. The users could build their own housing on this basis, thus participating in the design of their homes.

> "We soon came to the conclusion that to achieve that kind of hybrid, our strategy should combine two actions on the urban housing typology: hollow out and customize."

A few years later, and following Habraken's ideas, Frei Otto designed his Ökohaus in Berlin, where he argued that housing must always recognize two domains of action: the action of the community and that of the individual inhabitant. When the inhabitant is excluded, the result is uniformity and rigidity. When only the individual takes action, the result may be chaos and conflict. This formulation of a necessary balance of control had implications for all parties in the housing process, including architects, and it is in this sense that his project has proven to be more innovative. Here architecture can be understood as the formal representation of a sociological experience, which tried to reconcile the aspirations of all the final users.

> "What is important is the spatial innovation."

Recovering the essence of these experiences, in the RRURBAN project we try to work with basic volumes and standardized materials to reduce the final price. Because what is important is the spatial innovation. Hence, each housing unit can be easily adapted by the final users according to their preferences. A realistic "catalog of wishes" will determine the elementary characteristics of each "urban plot," which will be completely defined when occupying its final position within the general structure.

The disparity of volumes combined in height will promote the desired porosity, multiplying the system's adaptability to any site and generating a built environment of variable density composed by stacked basic volumes arranged to be inhabited. Among them, intermediate spaces are generated and treated as valuable extensions of the inner life.

The result is an inspiring as well as unusual collage of elements, a composition based on fragments representing the collectivity. Faced with the traditional neutral envelopes that give a unique and uniform image of the whole, in this case we can affirm that the façade is a sum of individualities and identities, a form of expression of the desires, aspirations and activity of each inhabitant—exactly what we were looking for.

TONY FRETTON ARCHITECTS

Westkaai Towers 5 & 6

Tony Fretton

PROJECT NAME
Westkaai Towers 5 & 6

ARCHITECT/S
Tony Fretton Architects, London / GB

BUILDING PURPOSE
Apartment housing

LOCATION
Antwerp, Belgium

CONSTRUCTION PERIOD
2013–2016

BRICK TYPE
Facing bricks

BRICK AWARD CATEGORY
Living together

BRICK 18 Grand Prize Winner

Situated along the Westkaai, six residential towers determine the new horizon of the northern harbor area in Antwerp currently under re-development. Old brick warehouses are being converted through multiple programs. Together with the new residential buildings, a mixed-used city quarter develops. This row of six towers has simply, but very effectively been divided into three pairs of buildings designed by different architects. The Towers 5&6 realized in this project by Tony Fretton in collaboration with De Architecten NV are the most northern ones.

They have a similar organization and height, but are slightly differently proportioned. Around a central access core the apartments are organized towards the façades, with balconies at each of the corners celebrating the panoramic view over the old harbor and adjacent historic city center. The most slender last tower stands slightly out of the building line of the others, thus giving an appropriate end to the new public promenade along the old harbor dock. The nuanced brick façades of both towers tie these new additions to the existing mix of monumental warehouses and mundane harbor buildings characteristic to this part of the city. The façades are a carefully proportioned grid of horizontal parapets and vertical piers that incorporates all windows and balcony fenestrations. The piers run to the ground, firmly anchoring the towers to their place. An elegant arcade mediates between the entrances of the tower and the public domain. It lends the building pair from a distance an abstract and monumental character that fits well within the context.

"The diversity and range of Flemish bricks allow a subtle color difference between the pair. Tower 5 is yellow and Tower 6 red, the classic colors of brickwork, but chosen in tones that make their color highly ambiguous."

To counter the repetition in the façades, a simple motif in the brickwork is introduced with a stunning effect. Originally load-bearing walls were constructed in a bonding of bricks laid in a length- and cross-direction. This bonding results in a vivid visual pattern of headers and stretchers. Since the façades of contemporary buildings are no longer load-bearing, they are constructed in a half brick thickness only. The resulting custom-applied stretcher bond of these contemporary façades lacks the visual richness of its predecessors. By re-introducing the old pattern of bonding, but simply shifting the cross-connecting brick in this pattern outwards, a decorative motif of projecting bricks occurs in the façade of the towers.

In the wider of the two towers, this projecting motif is employed in the parapets and lower part of the piers, thereby uniting them into a band that visually wraps around the building and emphasizes its horizontal proportioning. In the slender tower the motif is employed in the piers only to emphasize the verticality of this last tower in the row. The projecting bricks do not start from the ground, but gently appear as the pier of the plinth rises up. This persistent difference in horizontality and verticality is played out in the compositional ending of buildings on top, enhancing their difference. The towers in Antwerp display the experienced hand of an architect that controls both the overall monumental expression of a composition and much-needed variations so often lacking in contemporary housing through the sensitive use of a single material.

The residential towers by David Chipperfield Architects (left) and Tony Fretton Architects (middle and right)

Jury Statement

"We appreciate this project because it treats housing as an aspect of contemporary architecture and with normative programs in the city. It deals with questions of density, but also with a difficult legacy from a postwar period. It is important to recognize the qualities of this project, particularly the inventive use of brick. While the two towers work within the local tradition of brick housing architecture and at first glance appear simple in their formal language, more careful study reveals clear ideas in strategy and detail. We feel that the manner in which the use of bricks is explored in this project is in many ways radical, but it works with the surface and the manipulation of brick. It is not so much decorative, but it is strong in the exploration of brick as a material in its construction. The result is a most welcome contribution to the question of how housing can enhance the contemporary European city."

Façade design in detail ...

Site plan
1: Tower 6
2: Tower 5

... and in total view. The verticality is emphasized in the front tower, the horizontality in the back tower.

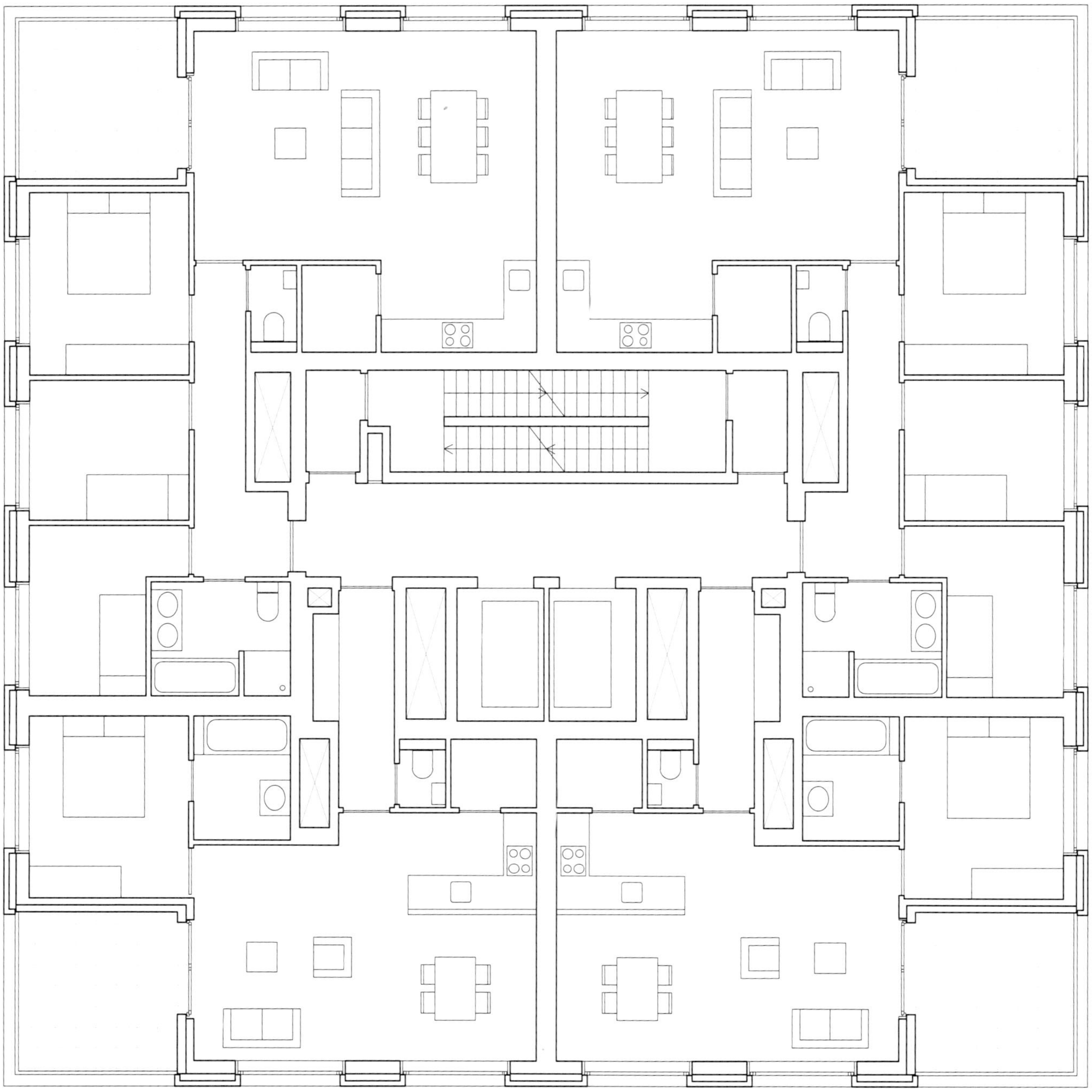

Tower 6, standard floor

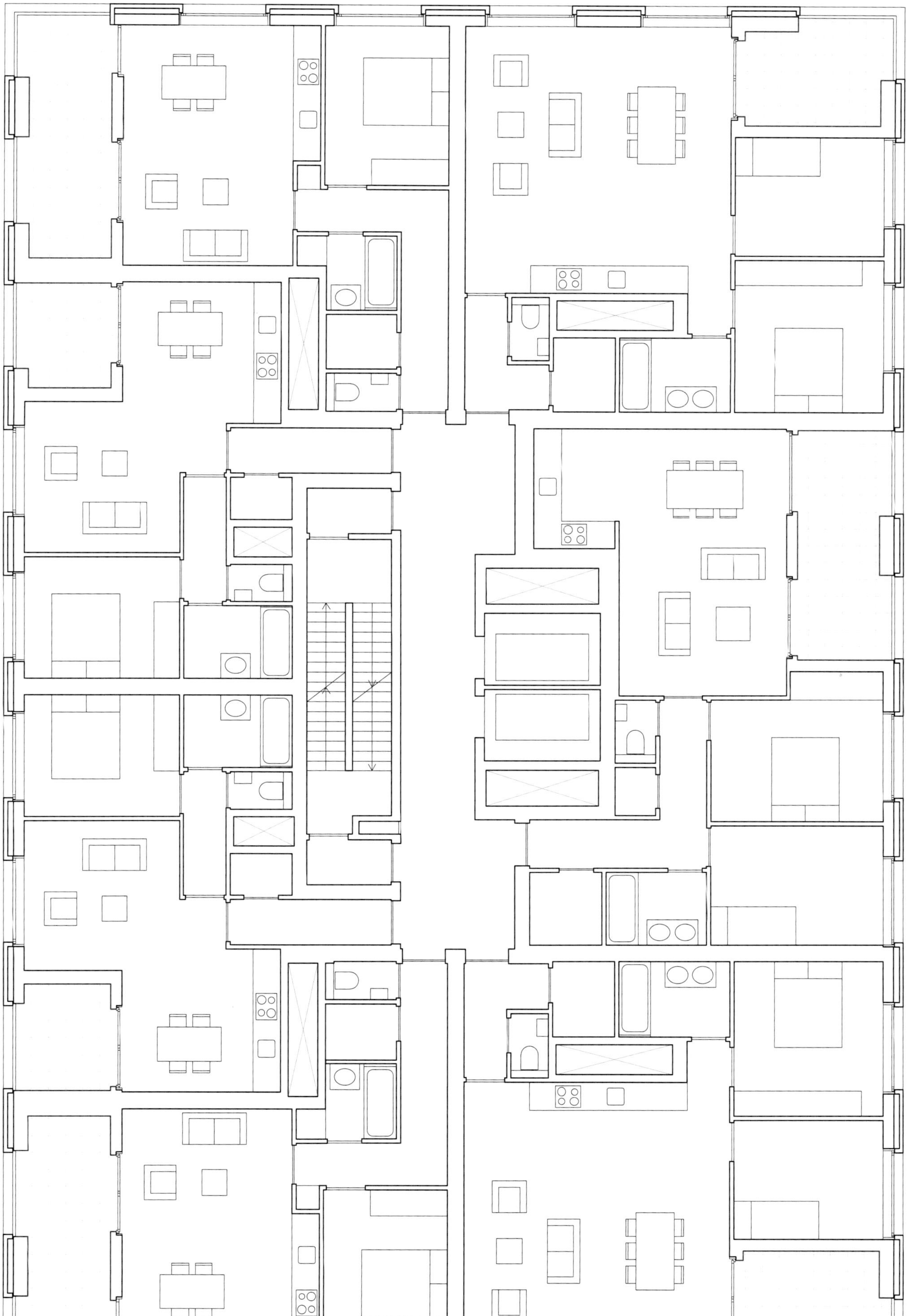

Tower 5, standard floor

DMVA ARCHITECTEN

Lorette Convent – Apartments Drbstr

David Driesen and Tom Verschueren

PROJECT NAME
Lorette Convent – Apartments Drbstr

ARCHITECT/S
dmvA architecten, Mechelen / BE

BUILDING PURPOSE
Apartment housing / offices

LOCATION
Mechelen, Belgium

CONSTRUCTION PERIOD
2014

BRICK TYPE
Facing bricks

BRICK AWARD CATEGORY
Living together

Situated half way between Brussels and Antwerp in the heart of the Belgian city of Mechelen, the property has a lively history behind it. The Hooghuys, an old merchant's house, counts among the city's oldest buildings and stands under UNESCO protection. Erected in neo-Gothic style in 1860, the adjacent Lorette Convent was used for almost 130 years as a girls' school and a nuns' congregation. In 1989 the houses were abandoned. For two decades, Mother Nature recaptured the area and gradually transformed the historic structures into a ruin. The condition was deplorable.

> "The white brick is an answer to the vitality and small-scale character of medieval Flemish houses."

In 2009, the decay was to come to an end. Hooghuys and Lorette Convent were sold to two investors, who revitalized and upgraded the property in the following years. The building wing along Begijnenstraat was converted into lofts and high-quality apartments. The row of houses on Drabstraat underwent a thorough restructuring and was renovated and extended by the local office of dmvA Architecten. Above all, the prominent lot on the rippling Dilje River was to be made pedestrian-friendly again.

The result of the extensive efforts is a sophisticated collage of old and new, of courage and respect, of conservation and commensurate reinterpretation. While the well-preserved structures were restored and the façade—along with the old anchor plates and the loose parts of plaster—was lime-washed, the architects placed three- to four-story urban fillings in solid construction with a forward-spaced brick layer into both gap sites. Bricks are laid—as is common in Flanders—in an irregularly staggered stretcher bond. The slender, but clearly emerging edging around the French windows is a demure reference to the old, partially three-dimensional, ornamented round arches and architraves.

"The white brick is an answer to the vitality and small-scale character of medieval Flemish houses," says David Driesen, partner at dmvA. "It was nevertheless important for us to generate a certain tension and to create a stimulating dialog between the individual building sections." Therefore, the monochrome new building was broken through at several neuralgic points with ground-level passages and ceiling-high loggias. Elsewhere, in turn, balconies and bridge-like additions slide out of the house. Vertical light strips, cut into the façade on the courtyard and street sides, are illuminated at dusk and light the open public space in this manner.

Not only does the revitalization of the almost 5,000 m^2-large area testify to an exemplary collaboration between two differently acting developers, but it is also a best-practice example for a modern handling of old locations. The ambience they created succeeded so brilliantly that the architects have decided to relocate their office and settle here. They couldn't have given their own project a more beautiful compliment.

Color gradations from the merchant's house, across the new building, all the way to the convent

The collage of old and new, seen from the inner courtyard.

Living together

View from Drabstraat

WILD BÄR HEULE ARCHITEKTEN

Apartment House with Industrial Brickwork

Thomas Wild, Sabine Bär and Ivar Heule

PROJECT NAME
Apartment House with Industrial Brickwork

ARCHITECT/S
Wild Bär Heule Architekten, Zurich / CH

BUILDING PURPOSE
Apartment housing

LOCATION
Uster, Switzerland

CONSTRUCTION PERIOD
2013–2014

BRICK TYPE
Clay blocks

BRICK AWARD CATEGORY
Living together

How does one, as an architect, provide for old age? By erecting an investment and subletting it to strangers until the point when one needs it personally. That's what the three architects Thomas Wild, Sabine Bär and Ivar Heule definitely did. In Uster, a community of 35,000 people near Lake Greifensee, they planned a three-family house that combines the duty of cost-effective building with the freestyling of beautiful living.

> "We wanted to show that such a small parcel can also be re-densified without harming the urbanistic identity of the quarter."

Located in the center of Uster, the house on Schöneggstrasse fits like a modern sculpture into the neighborhood development. Large window and façade surfaces characterize the building covered on all sides in concrete. In order to structure the volume, the architects decided to execute the façades in an alternately smooth and vertically fluted manner. Despite the hard building material, the house received a textured subtleness. A double-shelled wall structure with load-bearing industrial brickwork and internal, 20-centimeter-thick cavity wall insulation is concealed behind the striking envelope.

"A single-family house from the 1930s stood here earlier," remembers the architect Ivar Heule. "We wanted to show that such a small parcel can also be re-densified without harming the urbanistic identity of the quarter." The differentiation of the three apartments becomes clear by means of the exterior spaces: The ground floor is oriented towards the garden, a two-story loggia is attached on the first floor, and the maisonette apartment on the attic features two roof terraces with a view to the old city and the lake.

However, the house reveals its innermost values as soon as one closes the entrance door behind him/her. All walls on the interior were made of unplastered modular bricks. The characteristic industrial surface of the building material remained visible and was merely painted white. Depending on the sun exposure, an exciting play of light and shadow, changing hourly, emerges in the vertical grooves and flutes. At some spots even the lightly whitewashed production dates of the bricks are to be discerned. It is exactly this authentic rawness that lends the inner spaces their so distinctive warmth and feeling of security.

No chiseling work whatsoever was necessary. All the electric cabling was laid into the floor edges as well as behind the floor-to-ceiling-high door frames and window frames. The three apartments are warmed with floor heating installed under the rough-cut parquet flooring. Among all of this industrial bareness, poetry is not to be missed: the textile sun protection stores consist of embroidered insect fabric that casts tender shadow patterns into the room.

A very direct and nonetheless elegant materialization featuring the fine structure on the inside of the house

ROM.HOF Student Dormitory

Uwe Schröder

PROJECT NAME
ROM.HOF
Student Dormitory

ARCHITECT/S
Uwe Schröder Architekt,
Bonn / DE

BUILDING PURPOSE
Student residential
housing

LOCATION
Bonn, Germany

CONSTRUCTION PERIOD
2009–2014

BRICK TYPE
Facing bricks
Paving bricks

BRICK AWARD CATEGORY
Living together

At first glance one feels as if in a painting by the Italian artist Giorgio de Chirico. His colorless façades, his repetitive round arches, his often deserted streets characterized Surrealism and Metaphysical Painting at the beginning of the 20th century. The atmosphere here in the not-quite-so-cozy living area of Bonn-Dransdorf does not seem any different. The ROM.HOF appears prima facie bleak and forbidding, more reminiscent of a factory than a student dormitory. And the unusual brick building is also temporally hard to guess. Although erected just a few years ago, it could have been standing there for ages already.

"We are at the periphery of the city here and consequently at a location that is neither urban nor rural," says the Bonn-based architect Uwe Schröder. "From a design standpoint, it follows the classicistic university buildings in the Südstadt area of Bonn." On Siemensstraße the building emerges with three floors; on the courtyard side there is even one more on account of the sloping terrain. With its eleven arch axes, the fortress-like structure comes across as surreal and irritating.

The façade consists of reddish and ochre-colored, waterstruck bricks that were built up as a rear-ventilatefacing shell. Alternately making the stretcher and header sides of the brick visible, the wild bond breaks the hard rhythm of the window arches. While the plinth displays a high degree of red, the mixture becomes more ochre-colored and brighter towards the top. Schröder himself describes the organic progression as the "botany of the wall." That, however, not only takes poetry as a basis, but meticulous planning as well: the color, position and direction of every single brick were exactly predetermined.

"From a design standpoint, it follows the classicistic university buildings in the Südstadt area of Bonn."

Concealed behind the façade is a stringent, square floor plan with four stairwells in the corner and student rooms laid out in a ring-shaped manner, grouped around an inner arcade. Each of the altogether 93 rooms features a small loggia facing the street. While the room units are kept plain and neutral with wood and gray linoleum flooring, there is a sophisticated color code in the open areas and common rooms which dip the ceilings, depending on the position and function, in beige, blue, green and purple.

However, the centerpiece of ROM.HOF is the community facilities on the first floor and in the middle wing. At ground level there are water fountains and barbecue stations in both inner courtyards. The collective functions are housed in the slender middle wing: the canteen kitchen, the sports and game salon, as well as a two-story, sacred-seeming laundry room in which the socialization process at this stage in life manifests itself in the form of 14 washing machines and dryers lined next to each other. A stylized sun with 93 beams, which the Bonn-based artist Detlef Beer painted on the ceiling, hovers above. Seldom were art, everyday life and architecture so excitingly united as in this building.

Precisely planned organic color gradient

The round arches result from the constructive possibilities of the brick.

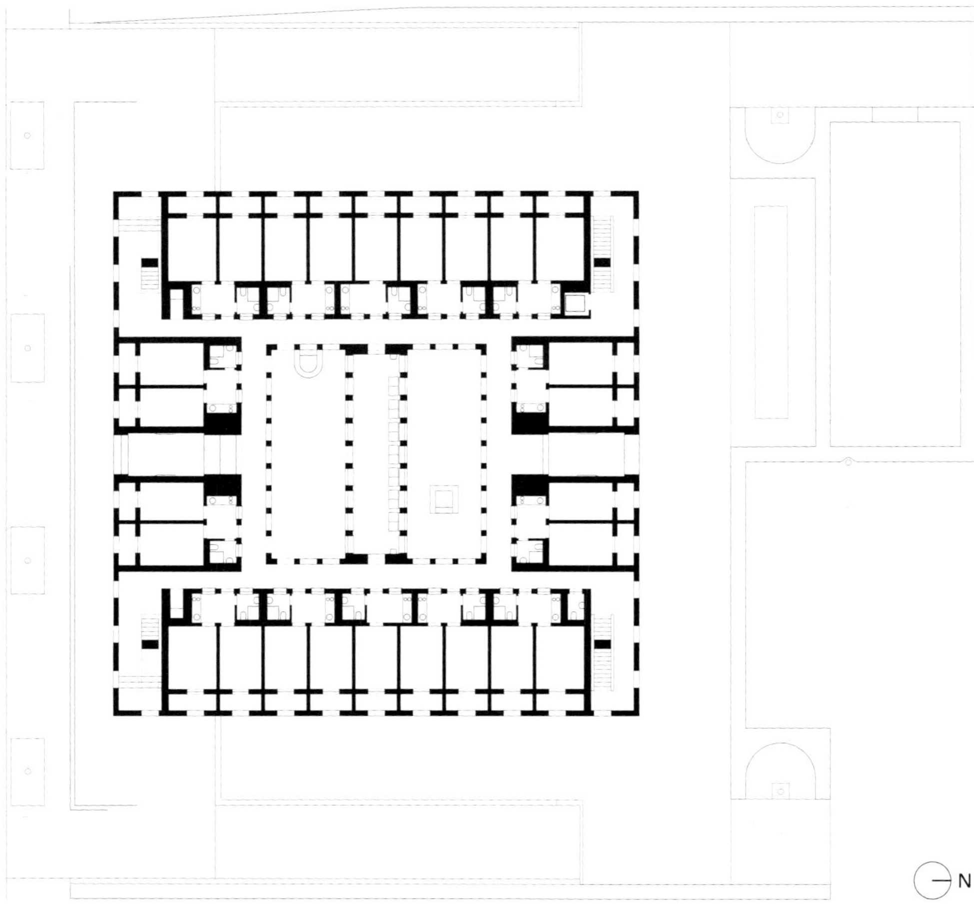

Ground floor

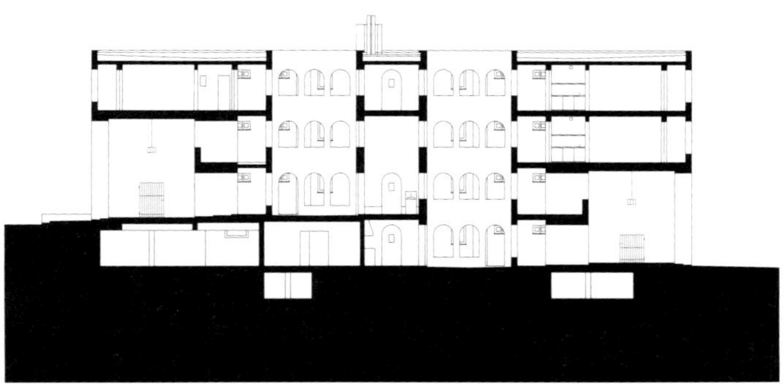

Section through the inner courtyards and the middle wing

VLA – VILHELM LAURITZEN ARCHITECTS AND COBE

Krøyers Plads

Thomas Scheel (VLA)

Dan Stubbergaard (COBE)

PROJECT NAME
Krøyers Plads

ARCHITECT/S
Vilhelm Lauritzen Architects, Nordhavn / DK and COBE, Copenhagen / DK

BUILDING PURPOSE
Apartment housing / retail

LOCATION
Copenhagen, Denmark

CONSTRUCTION PERIOD
2013–2016

BRICK TYPE
Facing bricks
Roof tiles
Brick slips

BRICK AWARD CATEGORY
Living together

The historic warehouses and storehouses in Copenhagen Harbor count among the most beautiful industrial areas in Denmark. Many of the brick buildings standing here are already 300 years old and have been converted into residential, office and cultural spaces in the recent past. Only Krøyers Plads remained untouched for a long time: Many project developers got engaged in the abandoned area directly situated on the water and proposed concepts that were all rejected by the local population. In the end, the decision was made to develop the 20,000-square-meter industrial compound in a participative and direct democratic manner and to involve the residents in the planning process.

"Thanks to the different bricks with their equally varied structures, we could react to the surroundings and prompt a dialog between old and new, between lightness and heaviness."

What resulted is a lively little piece of city, placed at the water's edge like a fine, carefully crafted filling between the Royal Danish Theater and Freetown Christiania. Three volumes soar up to six stories skywards and orientate themselves in terms of location, size and proportion to the surrounding development. The folded roof surfaces, which stand out like an angular hill contour on the façade, act as a slightly playful quote of the historic gables, dormers and little crane houses that have characterized the harbor from time immemorial.

Particularly sensitive is the choice of materials, since the architects decided to individually develop two completely different bricks and to carry the diversity of the location into the present in this way. In collaboration with a brick manufacturer, a shingle-like brick, which covers the entire roof landscape and parts of the façade, was produced. At a further traditional Danish enterprise, in turn, classic bricks with a cassette-like recess were selected. The irregular surface, spotted in various color shades, lends the project a vintage touch.

"The building material plays a central role in this project," Dan Stubbergaard, Founder and Chief Architect of COBE, explains. "We let ourselves get inspired by the red and ochre of the historic buildings. Thanks to the different bricks with their equally varied structures, we could react to the surroundings and prompt a dialog between old and new, between lightness and heaviness."

Krøyers Plads comprises 105 apartments featuring between 80 and 250 square meters of living space, numerous shops and restaurants, as well as a supermarket. The entire project was planned according to the principles of sustainability and resource conservation, which fall 40 percent below the legally stipulated energy threshold values. For the socially and ecologically unusual approach, the completed urban implant already received several awards at the beginning of 2016—among others, the Green Good Design Award and the Nordic Eco-Label.

105 apartments at the water's edge

The residents were involved in the planning process.

Two different bricks were developed for this project.

Folded roofs and architectural massiveness create a dialog between old and new.

STEFAN FORSTER ARCHITEKTEN

Philosophicum

Stefan Forster

PROJECT NAME
Philosophicum

ARCHITECT/S
Stefan Forster Architekten, Frankfurt am Main/DE

BUILDING PURPOSE
Student residential housing

LOCATION
Frankfurt am Main, Germany

CONSTRUCTION PERIOD
2014–2017

BRICK TYPE
Facing bricks

BRICK AWARD CATEGORY
Living together

For a long time things didn't look good for the Philosophicum. The eminent monument of postwar modernism had been erected at the Bockenheim Campus of Frankfurt University according to plans by Ferdinand Kramer from 1958 to 1960 and had housed the philosophy department. Nearly 80 meters long, nine stories high and 10.58 meters deep, the slab was one of the first buildings in Europe with an unclad exterior steel frame. Neglected by the university building department, it stood empty for a long time after the university had moved to another location and was to be torn down. But thanks to the protests of civil society, politicians and monument protection, the destruction could be prevented. A private investor ultimately had it renovated and extended by a five-story building along the road. 238 microapartments are now located in both houses; the offer in the new building is complemented by a day care center, a ground floor café and a roof terrace.

The architects see the new structure as an urbanistic corrective. The old building is set back from the street; like the exterior stairwells, the landings running along the outer wall are oriented towards the street. Erected upon a trapezoid-shaped plot, the new building completes the urbanistic structure and turns towards the public. It reflects the ground plan structure of the existing building: The apartments are oriented towards the street, the hallways lie at the back side facing the old building and dock onto the existing stairwells.

> "We are all especially happy about the 'new' façade of the existing building, which hardly differs from the original, and that we thereby succeeded in preserving a piece of Frankfurt postwar history and adding a new usage."

The façade of the new building adopts compositional elements of the existing structure and translates them into a distinct language. Resulting from the horizontal formats of the windows and the bright panels, the horizontal structuring of the Kramer edifice finds its analogy in the bright-sandy, circumferential concrete ribbons of the new house. The vertical structuring, which Kramer created through the exterior steel uprights, is incorporated into the new building through regularly arranged, vertical window formats; the clinker façade varies the colorfulness of the old building. It is kept in a light brown; the color of the bricks changes slightly so that the clinker surfaces are broken up in a diverse manner and are immediately recognizable as a brick façade.

Great care was applied to the restoration of the existing façade. The hope of being able to preserve it, however, had to be abandoned. Too extensive was the damage; the panels were only 5.5 centimeters thick and could no longer meet today's technical and thermal requirements. They were replaced by highly insulated, 18-centimeter-thick, lightweight metal panels. The windows were also replaced, the concrete slabs insulated on the inner side so that the hallways were somewhat narrower, but the outer appearance hardly differed from the original one. A happy end for the city, as well as for the friends of postwar modernism.

The street side with the new addition placed in front of the existing building

Gap between the two buildings

BARKOW LEIBINGER

Apartment House Prenzlauer Berg

Regine Leibinger and Frank Barkow

PROJECT NAME
Apartment House Prenzlauer Berg

ARCHITECT/S
Barkow Leibinger, Berlin / DE

BUILDING PURPOSE
Apartment housing

LOCATION
Berlin, Germany

CONSTRUCTION PERIOD
2015–2016

BRICK TYPE
Facing bricks

BRICK AWARD CATEGORY
Living together

An idiosyncratic apartment house has been standing in the inner courtyard of an apartment block in the popular Berlin district of Prenzlauer Berg since 2016. The shape—a cube and a high, truncated pyramid set on top of it—initially presumes the architects' extraordinary will to design. Yet the truth is rather different. It had been expected on the part of the historic monuments protection authority that the new structure orients itself to the house that had stood here until its destruction during the war. The separation distance regulations now valid would, however, not have allowed this. So the architects used the limits of what the regulations permit in order to generate this exceptional shape. Above the eaves height of 7.5 meters, the house rises over three stories with a 70-degree roof pitch and ends at a height of about 18 meters below the eaves of the neighboring house so that its firewall remains present. As a result, the new structure is clearly legible as an extension of a newer era, enhanced even more by the narrow shadow gap that sets the new house apart from the existing building.

Since the sloping surface actually had not been conceived as a roof and, on account of the steep pitch, is still readable as a wall, the architects placed the brick cladding over the entire surface. It changes direction without protrusions or recesses, runs over the roof edge and still covers the inner walls of the parapet and the floor of the roof terrace. The garden terrace in front of the ground floor was also paved with bricks. Distributed irregularly across the surface, the windows are flush-mounted into the façade and thereby intensify the impression of a clearly sectioned, closed structure. They are made of aluminum and were chosen by the architects to recall the often industrially characterized usage of such block interiors in the past.

"A unique character is created by this interplay of materials and production methods, the building appearing at the same time handcrafted and industrial, archaic and modern."

Although the shape, even if resulted out of the underlying circumstances, is an unconventional one that sets itself apart from the existing building, bricks that adapt to the environs were selected for the façade of the double-leaf construction. To this end, the architects incorporated the colors of the surrounding façades and created a range of six hues which the bricks were fired in: white, yellowish, orange, brown, pink-colored and gray bricks alternate with one other. Burn marks and handling traces were purposely left in order to ensure a diverse surface. Specially tapered bricks were produced for the sloping areas, the cornerstones are also custom-made. The façade was bricked in a wild, irregular bond; an applied slurry unifies the façade impression again in proportions.

Two spacious apartments, respectively organized as maisonettes, are located inside. An apartment with a garden and courtyard terrace extends across the first two floors; the three-story flat above it ends with a roof terrace.

Bricks extend from the garden, across the entire façade, all the way to the roof terrace floor.

E + N ARKITEKTUR

Mengel Tower

Kjeld Ghozati

PROJECT NAME
Mengel Tower

ARCHITECT/S
E + N Arkitektur, Aarhus / DK

BUILDING PURPOSE
Apartment housing

LOCATION
Aarhus, Denmark

CONSTRUCTION PERIOD
2015

BRICK TYPE
Facing bricks

BRICK AWARD CATEGORY
Living together

A city highway borders the northern edge of the inner city of Aarhus. In order to be able to build it, the houses on Nørregade, which had previously formed the edge of a city block, had to be torn down. One of the rows of houses, therefore, with a firewall toward the street, previously constituted the unsightly boundary. This transport planning wound was healed with a seven-story apartment building featuring 15 units.

"The Mengel Tower is a sculpturally formed building. This design is based on the desire for relatively cheap construction, yet boasts an engaging brick expression."

Following the new street line, the Mengel Tower, named after its builder, continues the line of the row of buildings with a bend inwards. At a special location on a busy street, but also at an exposed spot, the architects reacted with a composition of slabs running the full height of the building that do not meld into a closed form, but protrude as single walls in the space, lending the structure a defensive and protective quality, as well as an expressive presence at the same time. Some of these slabs are completely closed, others furnished with a few narrow, high windows reminiscent of crenels. Slight protrusions provide for vertical lines in the bends, which separate the single slabs from each other and therefore emphasize the compositional principle. Floor-to-ceiling ribbon windows, somewhat offset inwardly, lie between them. As a result, bright interior spaces emerged, despite the closed outward appearance. On the interior side of the block, facing eastward, the house comes out more open with balconies. They are situated so that one can sit here shielded from the glances of the neighbors.

"This special long brick format, together with the brick pattern, gives an appearance like a woven textile."

A special brick was used for the façade. Almost 35 centimeters long and 33 millimeters high, the reddish brick has a particularly flat size which finds little use today. Based on similar historical sizes, the manufacturer of these bricks calls them Roman bricks. The flat format requires that the proportion of the joints is higher in the elevation, thereby resulting in a characteristic, brighter image. At three places the architects pointedly applied the size: The extensive wall slab above the entrance is laid so that the bricks rotate out of the wall layer in a slightly slanted fashion, creating an especially lively surface. A row of vertically placed bricks respectively form the closure in front of the roof. And the slender front faces of the wall slabs are to be indicated as the third specialty. The slabs run conically towards their ends and thus appear narrower than they actually are in the middle. At this spot the right-angled bricks are intermeshed from both directions like a zipper. The resulting play of shadows accentuates the vertical and lends the house an aspiring elegance, despite its defensive character.

Living together

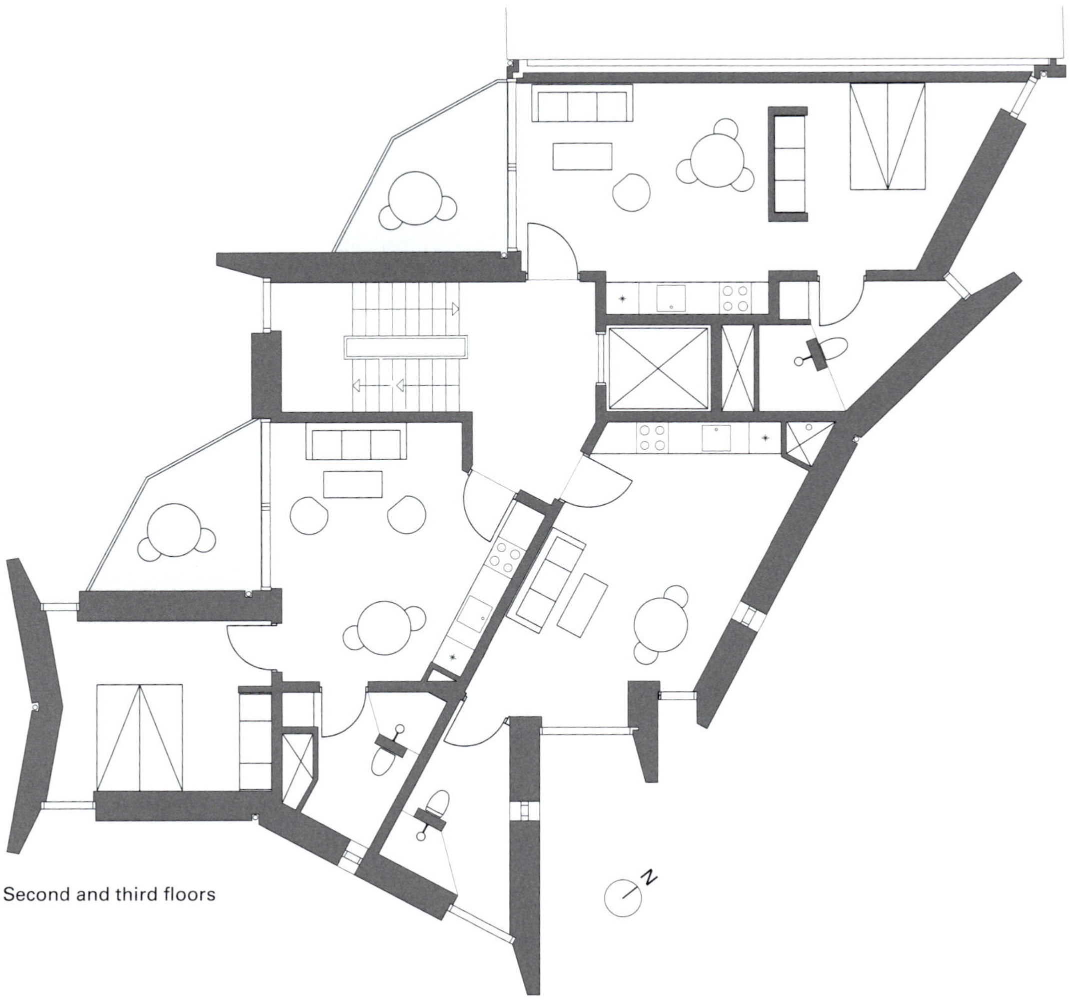

Second and third floors

Site plan

The Mengel Tower forms the conclusion of a perimeter development that is only fragmentarily preserved.

PRAKSIS ARKITEKTER

Carlsberg Researcher Apartments

Mette Tony and Mads Bjørn Hansen

PROJECT NAME
Carlsberg Researcher Apartments

ARCHITECT/S
Praksis Arkitekter, Troense / DK

BUILDING PURPOSE
Apartment housing

LOCATION
Copenhagen, Denmark

CONSTRUCTION PERIOD
2015–2017

BRICK TYPE
Facing bricks

BRICK AWARD CATEGORY
Living together

The Carlsberg district is situated in the southwest part of Copenhagen. The former brewery site will develop over the coming years into a mixed urban quarter with housing, amenities and cultural, as well as educational facilities. Witnesses to the rich industrial and research history of the place, the existing buildings are partly listed. At the border of the J. C. Jacobsen Garden the architects completed a new building that offers 22 apartments for academic researchers invited to work and teach in Copenhagen by the Carlsberg Foundation.

> "While usually rectangular, the production of bricks in fact offers a wide variety of shapes when molds are being adapted."

Orientated towards the park, the new building rises over a communally programmed ground floor with entrances and educational facilities. The volume of three to five floors with a setback on the lower part of the building responds to the various heights of the adjacent buildings. Organized around two staircases, the six apartments per floor vary in size and layout. Connected to the living room, each apartment has a loggia overlooking the garden. The rooms are finished to a high standard and detail, offering a warm welcome to the guests of the Foundation.

The refinement of the interior is mirrored in the exterior by the special use of bricks. While usually rectangular, the production of bricks in fact offers a wide variety of shapes when molds are being adapted. For the façade of the Carlsberg research apartments an angle corner has been cut away, allowing the bricks to be placed in a 45-degree, rotated bonding. The cut allows for a flat backside of the bricks to the insulation, hence offering a standard, cost efficient detailing. Every other layer of the bricks is turned in the opposite direction. This gives rise to a richly textured façade that offers an intriguing play of light and shadow over the ceramic surface.

At the plinth, the roof ending, the corners and around the windows and loggias, the bonding of the angled bricks transforms into a regular running bond with a flush surface. These transformations from textured surface to flush surface are designed with great care and result in a remarkable "reverse embellishment." In historic examples the reveals around windows, corners and cornices are usually subject to ornamentation and decoration in various materials. In the Carlsberg apartments the reversion with a textured façade surface and smooth edges brings about a contemporary interpretation of these classical architectural themes. It connects this new building to the historic surroundings while avoiding a mere copying of themes and, by doing so, opens a compelling perspective to the future development of the area.

The height development is oriented to the neighboring buildings.

Bricks laid in a 45-degree, rotated bond result in a lively façade ornamentation.

M3H ARCHITECTEN

Tugelablokken

Marc Reniers and Machiel Spaan

PROJECT NAME
Tugelablokken

ARCHITECT/S
M3H Architecten, Amsterdam / NL

BUILDING PURPOSE
Apartment housing

LOCATION
Amsterdam, The Netherlands

CONSTRUCTION PERIOD
2014–2015

BRICK TYPE
Facing bricks

BRICK AWARD CATEGORY
Living together

In the 20th century, the Dutch architect Berlage drew up the urban plan for the Transvaal neighborhood in Amsterdam, long before his well-known plan for the south of the city. The neighborhood's plan contains many of the characteristics that gave fame to Plan South, like the careful, at times picturesque layout of the streets and perimeter blocks, the incorporation of building ensembles into the plan and, of course, the use of brick in sometimes decorative fashion as the dominant building material. Along the train tracks that shape the northern edge of the neighborhood, five affordable housing blocks for Jewish craftsmen were built in 1915 according the design of the architect Leliman. These blocks of four floors plus an attic roof form an ensemble built on the same line along the street in an early Amsterdam School architectural style.

Within the ensemble, blocks three and four were recently demolished due to their bad technical condition and replaced. The aim with the new buildings was to provide apartments that meet the contemporary demands for accessibility for the elderly and to increase the much-needed mix of different lifestyles, incomes and ages in the area. In order to keep the integrity of the whole, both new buildings are carefully fitted within the existing ensemble in terms of volume and proportion. The new access typologies with elevators and deck access, as well as new car parking within the block, are craftily integrated. Taking a superficial glimpse, one would simply pass by these new buildings without noticing their presence.

> "The brick architecture and the application of art elaborate on the local building history without simply imitating it."

Upon closer inspection, however, the new buildings reveal an intriguing richness in bonding and colors of the brickwork façades. In line with the main composition of the original buildings, a variation of running bond, stack bond and even bricks on edge in tile bond is applied. This diversity enables the buildings to be scaled down and allows the repetition inherent to contemporary housing schemes to be balanced by a rich variation and human scale of the façade. In the existing buildings a colored tile tableau celebrating the original intent of the buildings is part of the façade. This tableau gave inspiration to an artwork by Atelier NL. The colors of the original tableau are used in the glazing of bricks that are applied in the façade as an independent, decorative layer. Not only do these decorative elements refine the architecture, they also resonate with the troubled history of these former Jewish houses. Overall, the project does not only display the possibilities of adding new housing typologies within the existing ensembles; more importantly the project shows a way of rethinking the rich brick history of the Amsterdam School in a fresh and contemporary way, avoiding the traps of nostalgia and mindless imitation.

The colors of this historic tableau provide the basis for the artistic intervention of glazed bricks on the façade.

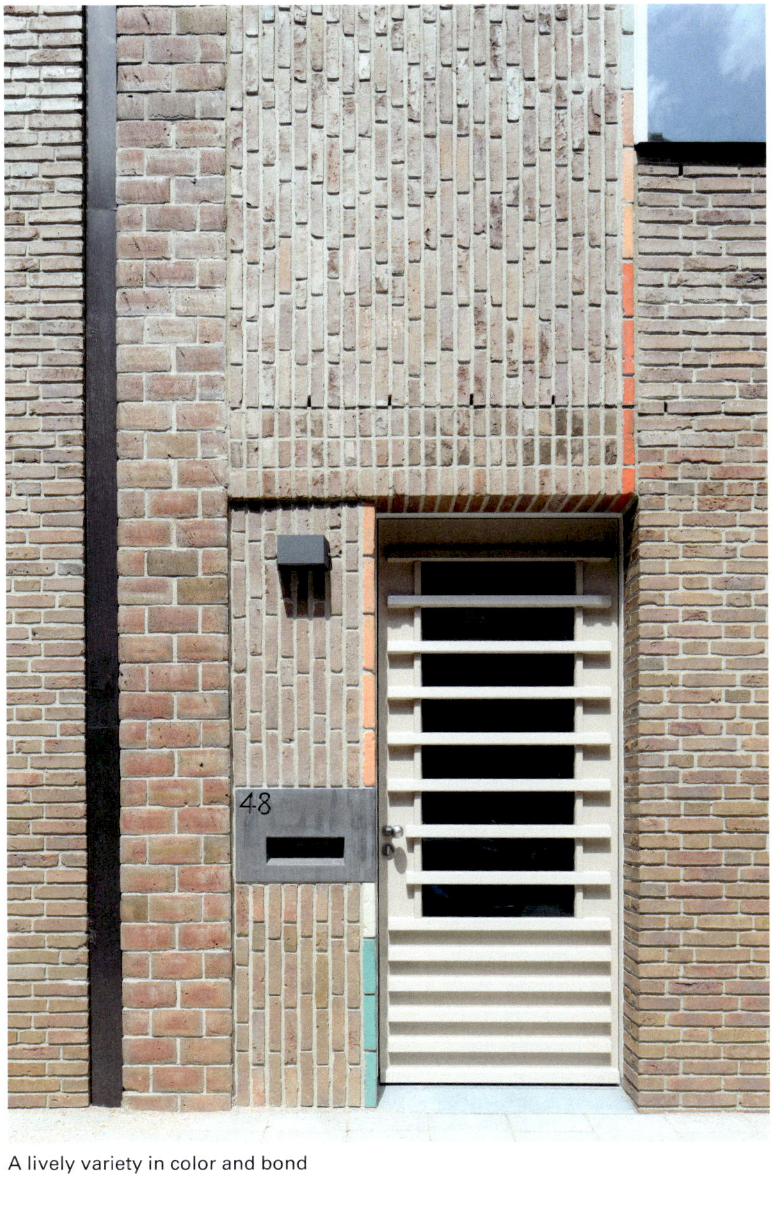

A lively variety in color and bond

Contemporary brick architecture that does not renounce the history of the location.

40
39

HANS VAN DER HEIJDEN ARCHITECT

Houses with Two Doors

Hans van der Heijden

PROJECT NAME
Houses with Two Doors

ARCHITECT/S
Hans van der Heijden Architect, Amsterdam / NL

BUILDING PURPOSE
Social housing

LOCATION
Rotterdam, The Netherlands

CONSTRUCTION PERIOD
2013–2015

BRICK TYPE
Facing bricks

BRICK AWARD CATEGORY
Living together

The Oranjeboomstraat is the main thoroughfare in the Feijenoord district in the south of Rotterdam. Once an avenue lined with trees on both sides and a tram running in the middle, the street has lost much of its urban grandeur. The individually parceled three- to four-story houses, churches and schools have partly been replaced by larger scale housing schemes ignorant of their historic context. The remaining houses have been renovated in such way that much of their original architectural refinements were stripped off. Recent social housing designed by the architects along the street shows a remarkable sense of place and history. It puts forward an alternative to the prevailing practice of generic and non-sensitive urban renewal that this district largely suffers from.

The project of 42 social houses fills a gap on both sides of an existing school left open after a failed larger urban development. In order to restore the rhythm of the street façades, a typology of stacked maisonettes is employed, resulting in a repetition of houses with two front doors. Car park and storage spaces are located in the back along a garden wall to a park and are accessible from the street through a gate that is an integral part of the architectural and urban composition. The ground floor of the lower part of the maisonettes is slightly raised due to the sanitation process of the polluted ground. Combined with the articulated roof endings, this results in an overall classical composition of the houses in line with their predecessors along the street.

> "A slight recess in the brickwork marks the division between the houses and lines of differently colored brickwork on the top support of the articulated roof ending."

Within the tight budget and standards of social housing, all possibilities that a brick façade offers are employed to enhance the urbanistic ambition of the project. The façades are made of standard-sized orange and light brown, hand-molded bricks. The bricks have been applied in random bond without butt joints and deeply recessed length joints, creating a horizontally textured surface. The colors are applied in a rhythm responding to the overall composition of the street façade. A slight recess in the brickwork marks the division between the houses and lines of differently colored brickwork on the top support of the articulated roof ending. A darker brick that is simply rotated and put in a stack bond creates the minimal plinth and bay windows. These bay windows vary in height from one to the exceptional three floors that emphasize the ending of the building at its angled street corner. The overall result is a rich composition of the street façade built up with minimal means. It displays the potential of how a modest material put into the hands of a sensitive architect can contribute to the much-needed design of the streets and cities that we inhabit.

The color and structure of the façades lend the apartment buildings a beautiful rhythm.

All of the details, right up to the railings, were carefully designed.

Working together

SANDY ATTIA

The Design of the Workplace

Sandy Attia

The office or, perhaps better yet, the workspace—office has a tinge of obsolete—is one of the most designed for and studied places in architecture, considering that it is not really a place specific to any one type of activity. An operating room in a hospital or the command center at the airport are places with a high quota of specificity and de facto design. Even though lots of work certainly takes place in these locations, their explicit functions circumscribe and limit their design. The workplace, on the other hand, is oddly generic and yet, generic is the last thing that the doctor prescribes for the welfare of the workforce.

Finding ways in which people at work can be happy, productive, creative and "connected" constitute a whole flurry of research and studies aimed at elevating the quality of the workplace. Offices today are a far cry from the elbow rubbing, sweaty spaces of our grandparents, and the alienating anonymity of the office cubicle has been surpassed by a decade or two. The open space workplace counterpointed the cubicle with a design solution that transferred ideals of equality and transparency in the call for a better work ethos, but it too has been subject to much scrutiny. The continuity and subsequent monotony of the open space created noise and privacy issues and was surprisingly no better at overcoming the dogged anonymity of the cubicle. So while the cubicle and open space planning produced similarly dull spaces, corporate office design sought out new strategies to animate the workplace. Catering to the employee's individual needs and providing all kinds of services that ranged from cafeterias, to gyms, lounges and grown-up play spaces, the corporate office created a new landscape of work. The design of the services, the interiors and the building themselves were intended to promote the corporate brand and to coalesce the workforce into loyal followers.

Corporate office design has since shed its initial Disneyesque flavor, maturing into a more refined version of itself. The emphasis on making offices fun turned into how to make them smart. The term "smart office" describes a data- and technology-driven workspace that simulates the human in such a way that the inanimate ensemble of building systems could not previously do. Striking the right light, temperature, humidity, and noise levels within the workplace during the different times of the day throughout the year was no longer simply the stuff of engineers, but rather a topic taken on by an interdisciplinary group of specialists: behavioral scientists, sound engineers, programmers and environmental experts to name just a few. From the aromas wafting through our air ducts, to the carpet beneath our feet, the office is a complex web of intricate design geared towards creating the perfect work conditions.

"The term 'smart office' describes a data- and technology-driven workspace that simulates the human in such a way that the inanimate ensemble of building systems could not previously do."

Beatriz Colomina and Mark Wigley, in their book titled *Are We Human?*, examine the omnipresence of design in our lives, and begin with the statement: "Design always presents itself as serving the human but its real ambition is to redesign the human."[1] In a certain sense, this is what the office environment is doing, it is retooling us; the architecture of the office appears to accommodate our individual work habits, but it is those very habits that the office is actually designed to modify. Be it the ergonomic chair correcting our posture, or the automated light shades recalibrating the dilation of the pupils of our eyes, our designed environment infiltrates our very beings. We not only see that design is everywhere, but that we, too, are designed as inanimate objects might be—thus the question "Are we human?"

The role of technology in the workplace has also facilitated new forms of how people work together. Co-working and office sharing are now diffuse practices, while pop-up companies that come into being for a single project are all products of our digital age. The space of these offices is less about architecture and more about networks of people. Like all networks, a network of people works only if the individuals of the group are connected to each other. This connection, however, is not only a digital or virtual one, but also a human one.

"The tectonic rigor of brickwork crystallizes a space nothing short of extraordinary, a beautiful place to work and feel good in."

Studies have shown that "feeling connected" not only makes you happier, but it can also add years to your life. *Mens sana in corpore sano*, sound body-sound mind (and vice versa), sums up the design trend of the workplace as a total environment. Out with the smart, in with the balanced, sensitive, "glocal" citizen as employee. The workplace, like the school, has become a place of learning, self-improvement and citizenship building rather than a place geared strictly towards efficiency. Meditation, mindfulness and environmental awareness converge in this new configuration of the workplace. Coaches, psychologists and color therapists attend to the inner workings of our mind to help us become less anxious and more at one with ourselves and the world.

"Like all networks, a network of people works only if the individuals of the group are connected to each other."

These lofty goals for designing for the "spirit" of those working are, of course, not new to architectural discourse. Frank Lloyd Wright in his design for the Johnson Wax Administration Building (1939) was fueled by the desire to provide an airy, light filled, collective workplace where people could thrive: "an inspiring place to work in as any cathedral was designed to worship in."[2] Coincidentally, the Johnson Wax Building is characterized by its brick construction. The almost singular use of red brick, together with the iconic columnar space of the Great Workroom, provide an unforgettable workspace—a place able to absorb change, a place able to stand outside of time. Indeed, the decision to design and build with brick brings to the fore the relationship between the materiality of architecture and its direct connotations on the workplace itself. The tectonic rigor of brickwork crystallizes a space nothing short of extraordinary, a beautiful place to work and feel good in.

1 Beatriz Colomina and Mark Wigley, *Are We Human? Notes on an Archaeology of Design*, Zurich: Lars Müller Publishers, 2016, p. 9.

2 Jonathan Lipman, *Frank Lloyd Wright and the Johnson Wax Buildings*, New York: Rizzoli, 1991.

Terra Cotta Studio

Tran Thi Ngu Ngon and Nguyen Hai Long

PROJECT NAME
Terra Cotta Studio

ARCHITECT/S
Tropical Space,
Ho Chi Minh City / VN

BUILDING PURPOSE
Artist's studio

LOCATION
Dien Phuong, Vietnam

CONSTRUCTION PERIOD
2016

BRICK TYPE
Clay blocks

BRICK AWARD CATEGORY
Working together

BRICK 18 Category Winner

In the rainy season, in the middle of the monsoon, the water in the Thu Bon Delta can already reach up to the house. But that doesn't matter. First of all, Le Duc Ha, one of Vietnam's most famous ceramic artists, can then take a break from work. And secondly, he doesn't have to worry about his thrown artifacts. Unaffected by the water, these namely rest a few meters above in one of the bamboo shelves separately made for this purpose. The concept for this originates from the South Vietnamese office Tropical Space. Their sensitive handling of the building material of brick is no coincidence. Already once, namely in 2016, the Ho Chi Minh City-based architects received the international Brick Award.

The Terra Cotta Studio is a 7×7×7-meter-large brick cube at the foot of the Thu Bon River. Hoi An, the world-famous, UNESCO-protected provincial capital, is just half an hour away by boat. The unusual perforation of the façade already attracts attention at first glance. Each lateral surface is respectively divided into 36 one-square-meter-large fields, which in turn are bricked in various bonds and allow different amounts of light and air to pass through in this way. The characteristic brick structure is a reference to the Champa Temple, which was erected around 1,500 years ago in this region.

"On one hand, this separating layer made of brick creates a certain privacy for the artist," says Tran Thi Ngu Ngon, who operates the award-winning architecture office Tropical Space together with her partner Nguyen Hai Long, and masters the tropical climate like the multiplication table. "On the other hand, the bricks allow some of the wind to blow through so that you get a natural breeze cooled by the river while working." Simple, yet efficient, the construction is the world's oldest and cheapest air conditioner.

On the inside, the façades—like a house within a house—are lined all around by seven-meter-high bamboo shelves. The 60-centimeter-large cubes, which cling to the brick walls like a wooden grid, serve as a gallery, as stairs, as well as an exhibition area for Le Duc Ha's artworks. A subtle steel construction with a glass roof hovers above it. "At least once a year there are floods in this region," the architect explains. "We have arranged with the artist to store his finished, but also unfinished works in higher-lying shelves at all times. In this way the floods cannot harm them anymore."

The center of the studio is a one-story, concreted table covered with bamboo mesh, which, as an archaic construction, separates the contemplative area from the busy one. While visitors go up in the mezzanine and can familiarize themselves with the works, Le Duc Ha sits on the ground floor at his potter's wheel, thus marking the geometric as well as the energetic middle of the house. Above a circular opening the sun shines on the clay and his hands. The light conditions change along with the weather and the time of day and therefore the working conditions at the wheel as well. Every moment is different.

"This separating layer made of brick creates a certain privacy for the artist."

Terra Cotta Studio is a place of concentration and creative abandon. It is a gift to the artist, but also to all those who yearn for a beautiful encounter with the material of clay, which is extensively celebrated here. An entire microcosm was created with very low construction costs. With this award the artisanal precision, the engagement with the traditions, and the conceptual strength of this extraordinary location take a bow.

Ancient temple buildings were the inspiration for the brick structure.

Jury Statement

"The building combines working production and domesticity. In our opinion, it somehow shows the future of working conditions. It is very special how this project uses brick in a traditional way in relation to climate and light. Furthermore, it is very interesting how history enters into a relationship with modernity—the past with the future. In this project brick is not something that has been put over the structure, but it is the structure itself, and it has also been used in the interior. The challenge was to connect the way of working and the way of using brick. Interesting is the relationship between how people work and how they live, because they live in a climate zone and brick influences the climate. The quality of the brick, the massiveness and the wind permeability of the material—the fact that wind can pass through it—can change the climate. So the building itself is very much related to the place and the way of working."

The façade fields are bricked in different bonds.

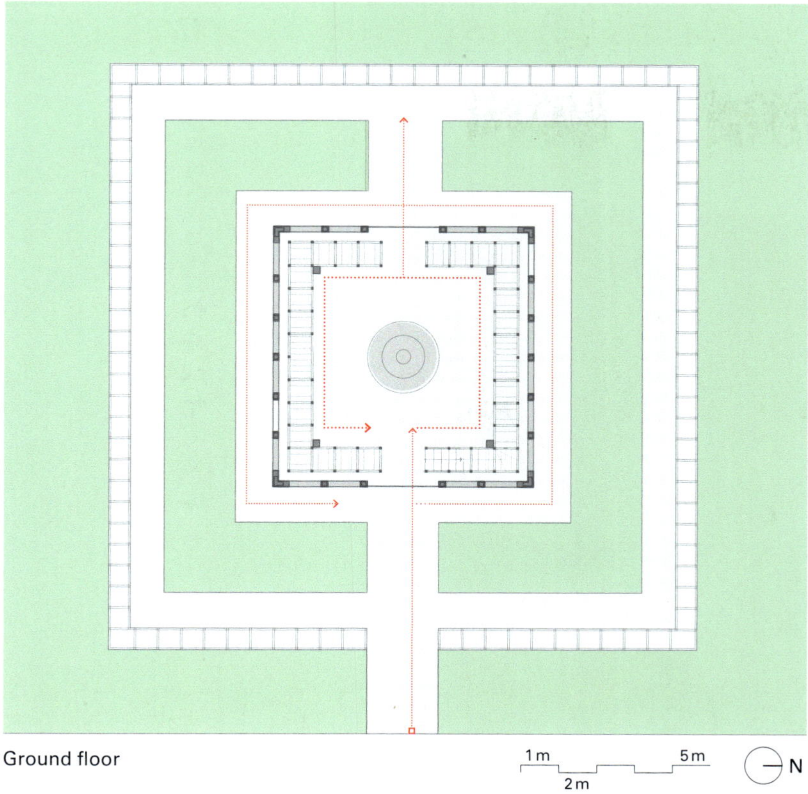

Ground floor

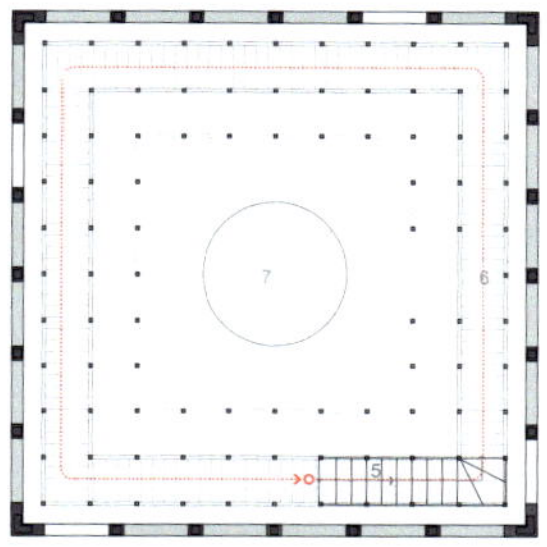

Second floor

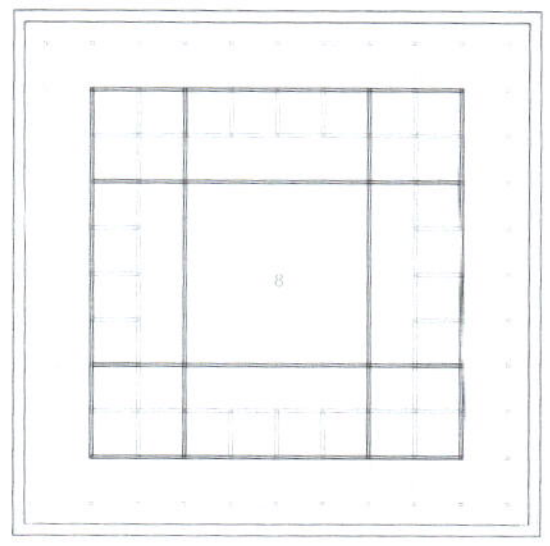

Roof plan

Working together

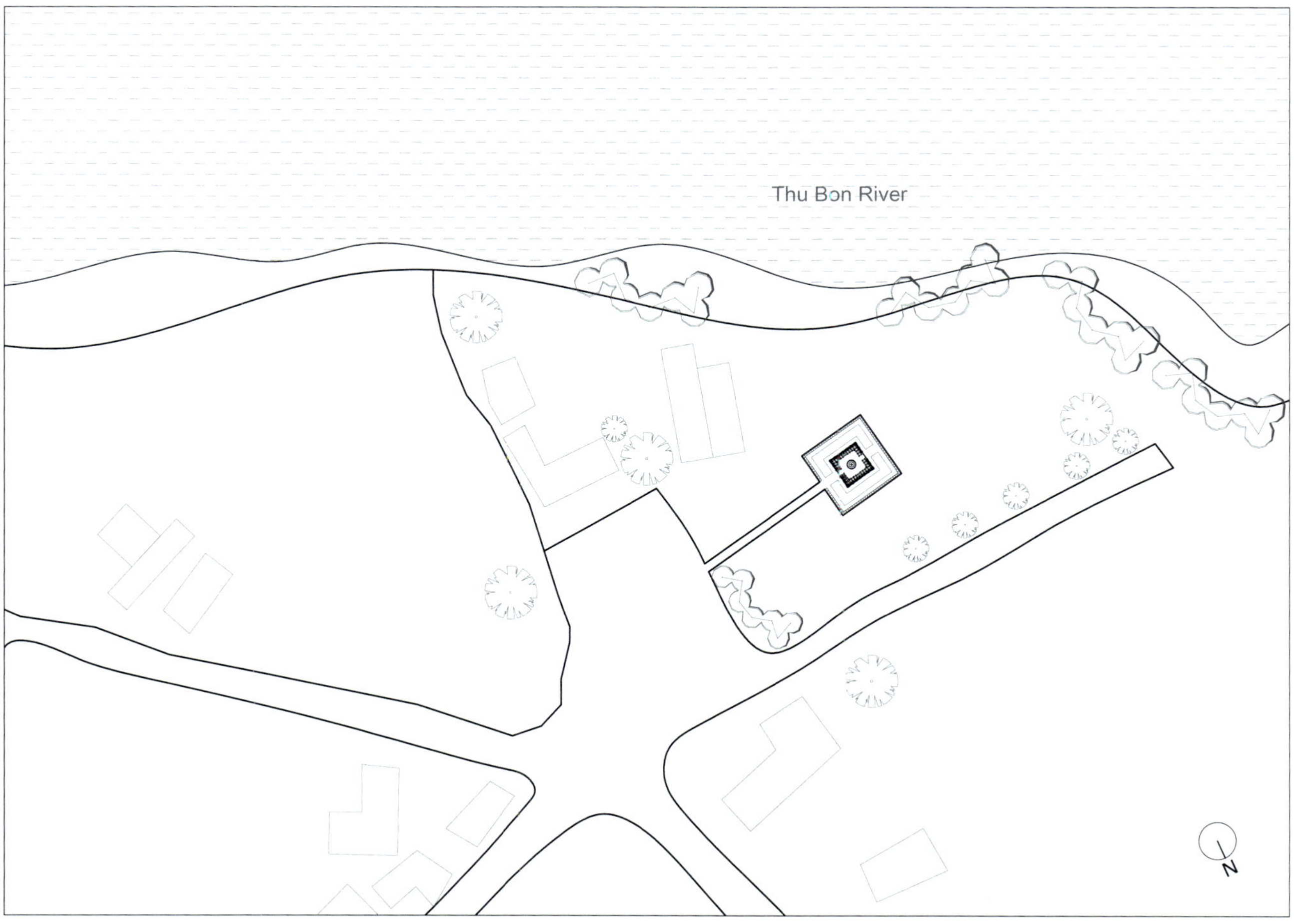

Site plan

The pottery wheel is the center of the house.

Within the brick structure there is an accessible shelf system made of bamboo.

HIERL ARCHITEKTEN

State Archives Landshut

Rudolf Hierl

PROJECT NAME
State Archives Landshut

ARCHITECT/S
Hierl Architekten,
Munich / DE

BUILDING PURPOSE
Offices / archives

LOCATION
Landshut, Germany

CONSTRUCTION PERIOD
2011–2016

BRICK TYPE
Facing bricks

BRICK AWARD CATEGORY
Working together

Since 1809, the Bavarian State Archives in Landshut had been located at Trausnitz Castle on the southern edge of the old city. This place didn't provide enough space any more and the climate conditions no longer corresponded to today's state of the art, so the partially sensitive archive material was damaged. Hence the decision was made to relocate the archive responsible for the administrative district of Lower Bavaria. The new storage facility for official books, documents, court records, maps and historical plans is now found on a corner lot in the north of the city which had been used up until recently as an allotment garden area.

> "In their arrangement and stacking, the clinkers are, however, a symbol for the storing of the archive material, too."

Hierl Architekten, a Munich-based office, proposed an L-shaped development with a plaza-like, urbanistically effective widening along Schlachthausstraße. At first glance, both of the 70-meter-long wings seem stringent and forbidding. Upon closer inspection, however, one recognizes the relief play in the façade structure with clinker bricks that protrude and recess. The visual appearance changes with proximity and distance: In detail, the different colors and sizes come across as chaotically jumbled; with increasing distance, a rhythmic order with a pronounced fishbone structure gradually comes to light.

"For the main part, the strongly horizontal façade tectonics are a reaction to the very long, linear shape of the building," explains architect Rudolf Hierl. "In their arrangement and stacking, the clinkers are, however, a symbol for the storing of the archive material, too. Like sheets in a pile of papers or files loosely stacked on top of each other, the bricks are an indication of the almost unimaginable quantity of archive material safeguarded here."

Around 65 kilometers of shelves, respectively, more than three million archive items, make up the store, which consists mainly of manually sliding mobile shelving. Various administrative rooms, as well as an own exhibition area that can be directly entered from the foyer, were added. Moreover, the two artists Hannes Arnold and Klaus-Dieter Eichler contributed their own art in architecture project. The glass installation "annu'ana" on the hallway walls is also partially visible from the street. "Here, the building type of the State Archives is less a simple store room, but rather a museum for profane cultural goods," according to Hierl.

Concealed behind the succinct façade shimmering in gray tones are 42-millimeter-high bricks cut into various lengths and widths, and fired in four different hues. The irregular waterstruck bricks with their characteristic surface were specifically developed for this project. And it was worth the effort: The bricks are as exceptional and unique as the files and books located behind them.

A fishbone structure emerges through the change in chromaticity, size and laying depth of the bricks.

The slender "Landshut steamed" brick was specially developed for the building.

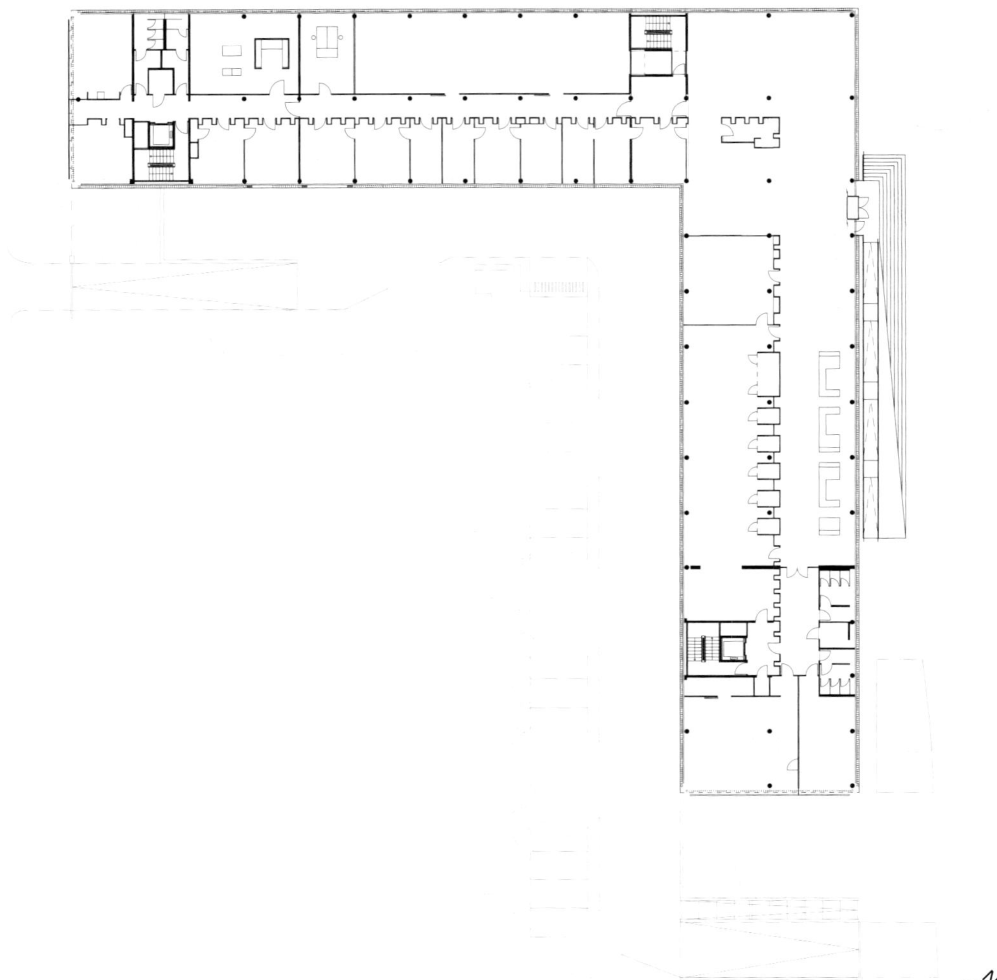

Ground floor

The strong horizontality underscores the shape of the building and, at the same time, is a reference to the paper stacked inside it.

DATA ARCHITECTES

CVAE Pantin – Sorting Facility

Léonard Lassagne and Colin Reynier

PROJECT NAME
CVAE Pantin – Sorting Facility

ARCHITECT/S
DATA Architectes, Bagnolet / FR

BUILDING PURPOSE
Infrastructure

LOCATION
Paris, France

CONSTRUCTION PERIOD
2015–2016

BRICK TYPE
Facing bricks

BRICK AWARD CATEGORY
Working together

Boulevard Périphérique around Paris counts among the most heavily travelled roads in Europe. At the same time, however, the city beltway, constructed between 1954 and 1973, is one of the city's largest structural barriers. 35 kilometers long, it separates the Paris suburbs and banlieues from the altogether 20 arrondissements of the metropolis on the Seine. The unattractive intersections above and below the highway, the bridges and bottlenecks, are reserved for motorized traffic.

"On one hand, our project is a small physical intervention; on the other hand, this intervention has big effects on the beauty and vitality of this urban space."

At precisely such a difficult "non-place," the Paris City Administration decided to start a pilot project and to erect a recycling and sorting center. The so-called "Centre de Valorisation et d'Apport des Encombrants" (CVAE) is located at Porte de Pantin in the northwest of Paris, just a few steps from the famous Parc de la Villette and Jean Nouvel's new Philharmonie, and is one of several waste logistics centers that are to be constructed in the coming years along Boulevard Périphérique. In collaboration with the architects, a bright, airy structure combining functional duty with aesthetic freestyling arose.

"Our goal was to utilize the space under the beltway in the best possible way and to give it a new task that precisely makes sense here," says Léonard Lassagne, Head Architect of DATA. "On one hand, our project is a small physical intervention; on the other hand, this intervention has big effects on the beauty and vitality of this urban space."

Between the existing bridge pillars, the architects defined a 1,400-square-meter-large area that they bordered with single-leaf, cross-bond brickwork. In order to let the construction appear lighter, the surrounding walls are executed with a concave, slightly curved contour. Selective recesses in the surfaces in the form of transparent glass blocks provide for sufficient daylight in the workspace below the bridge. Not least, the entire lot of bricks was glazed in a high-gloss white. That not only brought advantages in regard to cleaning, but also had an effect once again on the brightness and the emotionally felt cleanliness.

The recycling and sorting center is accessed on the east façade. There are clearly defined container spaces on the inside, as well as loading ramps and turning areas for the trucks. Following strict safety and logistics guidelines, the precise design was planned in coordination with the responsible city building division. As architect Léonard Lassagne says after all: "These are exactly the challenges and difficult underlying circumstances that spur us planners on and lead to innovative solutions and concepts that recycle the city and make it come alive in a new way."

White lacquered bricks are easy to clean and provide for a bright, clean atmosphere.

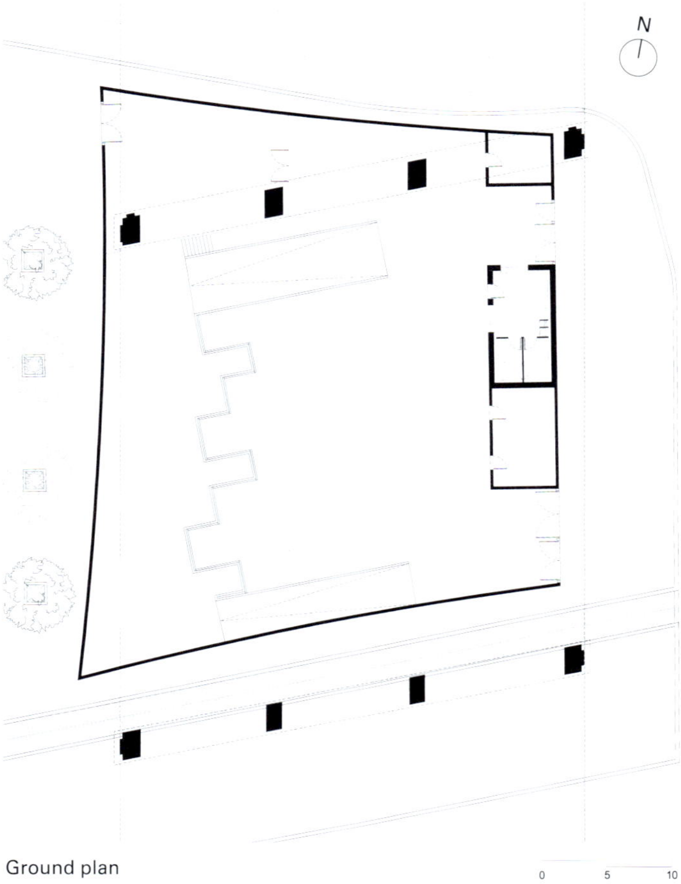

Ground plan

The subtle design of the brick wall upgrades the location in an aesthetic and atmospheric respect.

LRO LEDERER RAGNARSDÓTTIR OEI ARCHITEKTEN

Sparkasse Ulm

Marc Oei, Arno Lederer and Jórunn Ragnarsdóttir

PROJECT NAME
Sparkasse Ulm

ARCHITECT/S
LRO Lederer Ragnarsdóttir Oei Architekten, Stuttgart / DE

BUILDING PURPOSE
Offices

LOCATION
Ulm, Germany

CONSTRUCTION PERIOD
2013–2015

BRICK TYPE
Facing bricks

BRICK AWARD CATEGORY
Working together

The new building of the Sparkasse Ulm stands at the edge of the historic inner city, near the Ulm Minster. Its immediate opposite is the "Neuer Bau," a mighty brick building from the 16th century, which, together with the new Sparkasse bank building, forms the entrance to the "Neue Mitte" ("New Middle"). An exemplary city renovation project, the Neue Mitte arose between 2002 and 2007 as a new development on a thoroughfare cut through the inner city after the war, the Neue Straße.

The architects faced the task of designing a building that corresponds with the "Neuer Bau," but at the same time self-consciously articulates itself as a product of the 21st century. They solved this with an architecture of expressive elements. A high colonnade lies between the street and the building wall as a filter; the office stories above are folded outwards in a zigzag pattern and ribbon windows placed around the corners are equipped with polished stainless steel frames. They develop a special effect in the external view, since the surroundings are reflected in them like a kaleidoscope. But these windows enrich the interior, too: They provide light and expanse; after all, the view is not only possible straight ahead, but also to the right and the left.

The facing shell of this expressive structure consists of recycled bricks in a bright, earthy tone. These bricks basically ensure a lively, diversified surface. The width of the bricks varies between 8 and 11.5 centimeters, but this is not obvious due to the good work performed by the executing firms. The idea of longevity and sustainability is implemented here in a two-fold way: through bricks as robust and enduring building material and as recycled material.

> "On account of our experience with used bricks, we could convince the client about the advantages of the old brick. Not only due to the correspondence to the historical façade, but also because the recycling of demolished building material represents an important topic in the sustainability and consideration of material cycles."

A special detail is found on the front façade pointing westward: round, tilted slabs covered with special terracotta-colored bricks discretely guide glare-free natural light into the interior of the corridor zone situated in the middle as reflectors.

Towards the south, where the terrain slopes, the Sparkasse building is lower. Through this staggering, the building withdraws at this spot and thereby blends into the adjacent urban context here as well. This attention is also distinctive for the quality of the whole: The back side is not neglected in favor of the visible side.

The building as an expressive kaleidoscope

Recycled brick was used for the project.

MAX DUDLER

Reception Building Dräger

Max Dudler

PROJECT NAME
Reception Building Dräger

ARCHITECT/S
Max Dudler, Berlin / DE

BUILDING PURPOSE
Offices

LOCATION
Lübeck, Germany

CONSTRUCTION PERIOD
2013–2015

BRICK TYPE
Facing bricks

BRICK AWARD CATEGORY
Working together

Dräger, a company based in the Hanseatic City of Lübeck, was founded in 1889. As a producer of devices and systems for medical and security technology, the firm equally sees itself as being aware of its tradition and oriented to the future. The new office building marking the entrance to the company premises expresses this in a very pointed fashion—its brick façade references the expressionist architecture of the 1920s, the large windows showcase the modernity of the building. The new structure replaces an old factory gate that previous stood here. Now it functions as the firm's new and impressive calling card.

Completed in 2015, the reception building, along with two further structures from different eras of the company's history, fills a place that consequently represents the history of the enterprise up into the 21st century. The new construction is a composition of five-, six- and eight-story components that elegantly connect to the existing stock. The lower ones attach to the older structures and segue into an eight-story head building which prominently accentuates the corner. This head building orients itself towards the square, projects into it; a two-story-high colonnade gives the square an urban flair. The pillars and beams of the steel frame structure were clad with 115-mm-thick clinkers that cover the façade like a grid. The triangularly tapered pillars emphasize the verticality.

"The upper building envelope of the structure is accentuated by a fold that lends it an expressive crown. These details of the clinker façade mark the design as an interpretation of Northern Germany's architectural tradition."

On one hand, the façade makes reference to the brick architecture of Lübeck's old city, on the other hand, to Northern Germany's Brick Expressionism developed in the early 20th century, which is taken up again in a clearly visible manner here. Star-shaped corner pillars show this reference in a particularly distinct way. On the lower six floors, the large, floor-to-ceiling, frameless windows create the impression that a single, continuous, glass surface would lie behind the façade, thus especially highlighting the brick structure. The window surfaces and the horizontal brick strips are bent inwards so that the building concludes like a crown.

The waterstruck bricks used were produced by a traditional process in a coal-fired kiln, which lends them a rough, diversified and workman-like character. This special singularity of the bricks develops by pressing the clay through a mold with water, causing the water to subsequently react physically with the clay and the air, giving each brick a distinct surface.

"The large, abstract glass surfaces stand for the company's orientation to the future, while the rough waterstruck bricks, as a traditional material, emphasize the long company tradition at this location."

One reaches a high, two-story foyer, which functions as a reception room for visitors and employees, via the colonnade. The offices, where about 200 people work, are accessed from here. Company executives toil on the upper floors, which offer a superb view of the company compound and the city.

The verticality of the building is accentuated by the triangular pillars.

The grid structure of the construction transforms into a "crown" on the top two floors.

FLORIAN NAGLER ARCHITEKTEN

Keep it Simple – Studio, Workshop and Depot

Florian Nagler

PROJECT NAME
Keep it Simple – Studio, Workshop and Depot

ARCHITECT/S
Florian Nagler Architekten GmbH, Munich / DE

BUILDING PURPOSE
Working space

LOCATION
Gleißenberg, Germany

CONSTRUCTION PERIOD
2013–2014

BRICK TYPE
Clay blocks

BRICK AWARD CATEGORY
Working together

The new construction for the artist Peter Lang consists of three halls of the same height and width, but which slightly differ from each other lengthwise in a somewhat offset manner, making each of the three structures well distinguishable. This simple spatial concept is reflected, on the one hand, in the interior structure: One hall serves as a depot for paintings, the second functions as a workshop and the third as a painting studio. On the other hand, the ensemble blends into the village context in a suitably scaled manner through the three-part division. The gabled roofs, the coarse plaster and the large gates, like those also found on barns, likewise forge a link to the local building tradition. Gleißenberg has around one thousand inhabitants and lies close to the Czech border in the Upper Palatinate region north of the Danube. Therefore, the cubature also makes a reference to the old glass manufacturers that are part of the regional building history.

As simple as possible was the maxim of the design and execution. Simple not only in the appearance and materials, but also in the construction methods familiar to every tradesman. And not as an end in itself, but in accordance with the usage requirements: For the storage of his pictures, the artist desired an indoor climate similar to that of an old church. This wish was fulfilled through a solid wall construction, a large, unheated room volume, and a low proportion of window area, so that the interior room climate slowly adapts to the outside temperature fluctuations and the moisture content remains stable.

For the entire construction, the architects chose a single-leaf structure made of highly insulating bricks covered on the outside with a coarse, gray-colored plaster. The interiors of the workshop and studio were coated with white slurry; the depot walls remained untreated on the inside. The few window openings—the walls of the depot are completely closed—are fixed-glazed; the floor consists of a smoothed slab made of steel fiber concrete; an open construction with white-varnished wooden trusses was selected for the roof. Skylight strips across the ridge line were covered with polycarbonate panels, the closed roof surfaces with sanded bitumen sheets. A large concrete beam between the studio and the workshops enables the spatial boundary closed by a mobile cabinet wall to be opened, creating an over 400 m² space.

"The used constructions and materials are extremely simple. The goal was to design as few details as possible."

As subtly and discretely the buildings may also differ from a common commercial construction through the care given to detail—should they one day not to be used any longer by Peter Lang, they are also precisely suited for such purposes, for instance, for a carpenter's workshop; the interior spaces, for example, can also be accessed by a small truck from the street. It is not least this pragmatism that makes this ensemble stand out as one typical for rural construction.

As simple as possible: brick masonry with a rough, bright plaster

The trichotomy ensures that the village-like scale is preserved.

The large gates recall those of the barns in the surroundings.

By opening one large sliding door, the studio and workshop can be connected to each other.

BUREAUVANEIG

't Melkhuisje

Marjolein van Eig

PROJECT NAME
't Melkhuisje

ARCHITECT/S
BureauVanEig, Rotterdam / NL

BUILDING PURPOSE
Infrastructure

LOCATION
Haarlem, The Netherlands

CONSTRUCTION PERIOD
2015

BRICK TYPE
Facing bricks

BRICK AWARD CATEGORY
Working together

t 'Melkhuisje is a new bridgekeeper and electricity house along the Melkbrug ("Milk Bridge") in the historic center of Haarlem. It stands in a long tradition of small utility buildings located in the city. Often designed in series, they slowly lose their function due to scale enlargement and digitalization. This new bridge house is a positive exception to this development and highlights the urban and architectural potential of these buildings.

> "The building shows four different façades, which makes it fascinating and intruiging. It invites to come and have a closer look."

The "Milk Bridge" forms a pair with the "Catherine Bridge," connecting the eastern and western part of the historic center of Haarlem. Both bridges are cast iron constructions with Neo-Renaissance characteristics and are listed monuments. Built upon the existing foundations, 't Melkhuisje replaces a control building from the 1960s which was damaged by a fire. The small structure contains a power transformer station and a touristic information point next to the control room for the bridge operator. The required space for the transformer and information point determined the volumes of the lower part of the building. A steep, asymmetrical pitched roof crowns the slender volume for the bridge operator. It protects the control room from the sun and balances the "belly" of the lower part.

> "The bricks are laid in relief, thus creating a surface which changes throughout the day by the sun causing different shadows on the surface."

This characteristic volume that reads differently from all sides plays upon the archetypical house with a roof. The entire façade and the steep part of the roof are clad in a brown brick that protrudes outwards every other layer. The use of brick familiarizes the building and ties it strongly to its surroundings, since Haarlem is a city built in brick. Moreover, the green steel elements refer to the color of the bridge that it serves. The texture of the brick pattern lends the slightly awkward volume richness in the play of light. 't Melkhuisje fits perfectly to the site and addresses in a sensitive manner the rich tradition of utilitarian objects that light up our cities when made with care and attention to details.

The little house sets itself distinctly apart from the surrounding area through its special brick structure.

A whole half house

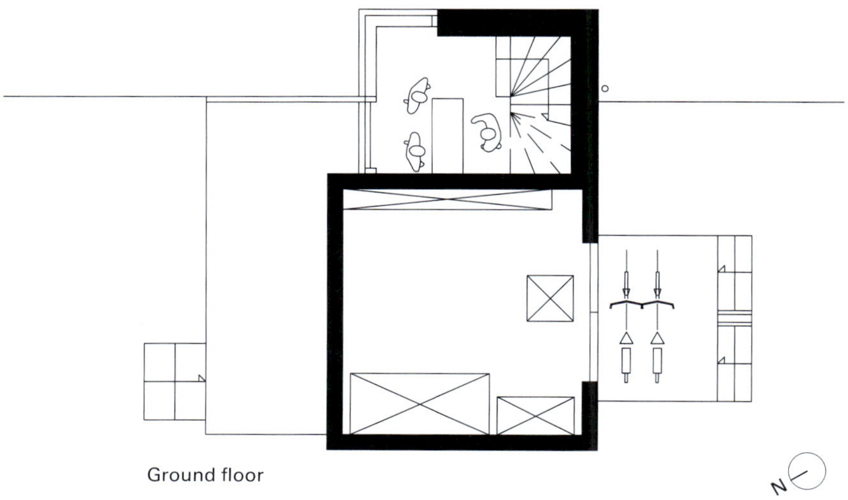

Ground floor

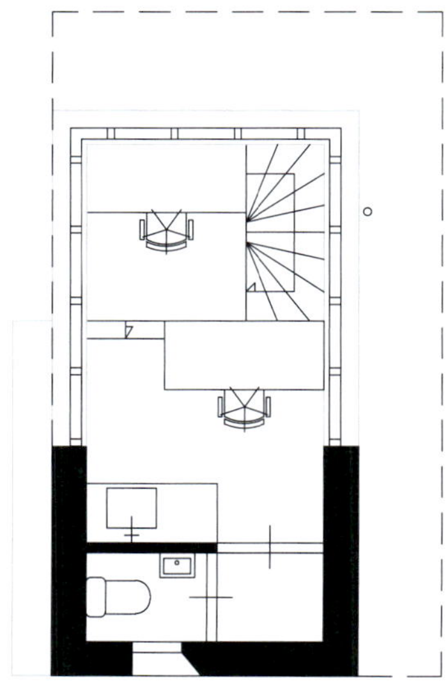

First floor

Pavilion Brick Factory Vogelensangh

Thomas Bedaux, Pieter Bedaux and Joyce Verstijnen

PROJECT NAME
Pavilion Brick Factory Vogelensangh

ARCHITECT/S
Bedaux de Brouwer Architecten, Goirle / NL

BUILDING PURPOSE
Offices

LOCATION
Deest, The Netherlands

CONSTRUCTION PERIOD
2016

BRICK TYPE
Facing bricks

BRICK AWARD CATEGORY
Working together

The Vogelensangh brick factory along the Waal River contains the last remaining coal-fired ring kiln in the Netherlands. The factory has been operating since 1919 and after a restart in 1988 the fire has been running its perpetual circle in the kiln, taking around 14 days to fire the bricks. The kiln itself is a listed monument and produces a rich variety of hand-molded bricks with a nuanced color palette characteristic to this type of kiln.

> "The bricks produced on site have purposely been laid in a simple bond that refers to the rational way bricks are stacked during fabrication."

At the entrance of the site the architects designed a new office and reception pavilion for this historical factory. This resulted in a design that, both in its exterior and interior, emphasizes the timeless beauty of the tradition of hand-shaped bricks.

The pavilion stands slightly elevated on a platform and elegantly separates a "clean" welcome area with parking and entrance from the muddy production grounds. Towards the entrance the pavilion presents itself with a closed surface giving expression to the building mass and the bricks it has been constructed from. The characteristic red bricks produced on site are applied in a thinner than usual size (Vecht size) with deeply recessed bed joints and no butt joints. The loose bonding recalls the way bricks are stacked when produced. Small windows towards the service areas are hidden behind a decorative pattern of bricklayers, while the entrance door itself is deeply recessed within the building mass. The unity of retaining walls of the platform and the façade emphasizes the ceramic, robust character of the pavilion and announces the world of bricks one is to enter.

> "All in all, a pavilion that is closely related to its environment, not only designed for, but also materialized with and inspired by the client."

The pavilion itself is separated in length by a closed entrance and service zone and an office and reception zone offering a stunning panoramic view over the factory grounds and the monumental kiln. Contrasting with the warm red outside, all interior walls and vaulted ceilings are constructed in a pale yellow brick, lending the interior a slightly understated, refined character. The enfilade of office and reception rooms is united under a vaulted roof reminiscent of the vaulted chambers of the factory's ring kiln.

The slender brick in stretcher bond contributes towards emphasizing the horizontality.

Reception building of the historic brick factory

The brick is produced on-site and bricked up with deeply recessed bed joints and without butt joints.

Yellowish bricks were used on the interior of the pavilion.

Sharing public spaces

PATRÍCIA BARBAS

Sharing Public Spaces: Strangely Familiar

Patrícia Barbas

In these times of blurred realities and globalization what is public and what is private? And what are spaces either public or private? Despite uncertainty, I still think public spaces are places where we coexist, not as avatars or digital profiles, and where we can be at the same time both actor and anonymous bystander. The city's logic is timeless. From the Greeks' Agora or the Romans' Forum, public spaces are still the scene of the main episodes of public life and the expressions of the character of its inhabitants, besides the continuous changes of technology and media that transform the way we live, work and travel. Public spaces, in their physical and symbolical dimension—and within a context of virtual relationships, far from becoming obsolete—have an important role in the city's existence.
No matter how much we live virtually (informed or misinformed) through social networks, the places for reunion, trading, manifestations or representations are still the public spaces in the city. Cities are about people, citizens and "real" life taking place in "real" places.

In 2015 we were awarded the project for an office building in Lisbon. The design was selected through a closed competition between seven architectural teams that was coordinated between the developer and the municipality. They did not just want a building, they wanted to design a solution for the complex urban tissue which surrounded the plot. Avenidas Novas, the 19th century expansion of Lisbon on the north side, is the new location. The plan for these "new avenues" appropriated principles and techniques of progressive urbanism which the Parisian boulevards were the references for. But, differently from Paris or Barcelona, the old city of Lisbon was not in question, since its development had been planned through enlargement rather than reconversion. Unfortunately, the quality of the buildings did not correspond to the urban plan, since they were extremely heterogeneous, manifesting the economic and social fragility of the Portuguese bourgeoisie.[1] Prior to 2016, the area was a blend of different eras, and cars had conquered the public space. Thereafter, a program called "one plaza for each neighborhood" was implemented by the municipality to create new public spaces, where micro centrality and soft modes of locomotion are privileged.

Our proposal was to design the office tower in the corner of the plot and free up space on the avenue level for public use. This simple gesture fits between two different epochs, the romantic idea of the 19th century Lisbon, such as the Anastácio Gonçalves House Museum, and the modern Lisbon, such as the 70's project for the Sheraton Hotel and the Imaviz shopping mall and residences. The design of the square and new gardens is able to redefine elements and backgrounds connecting the building to its surroundings—the neighbors' alignments and topographical differences—and provide the guidelines to transform the space for public enjoyment.

> "No matter how much we live virtually (informed or misinformed) through social networks, the places for reunion, trading, manifestations or representations are still the public spaces in the city."

The office building is a quite important typology in contemporary societies. Constructive rationality, layout flexibility, environmental comfort or good energy performance are central aspects of the project. An office building is a machine, complying with legal regulations and technical standards to satisfy the profitability of an investment. Architecture fulfills this desire to create commercial value and a qualified real estate offer. However, an office building is much more than that. It is a large-scale urban element impacting both physical and social environments. It attracts many people and transforms the city's image. Despite being private as a mission, it has a strong public expression.

What interested us was this possibility of transforming the place through a hybridization of public and private spaces and by not being able to precisely define the boundary which separates public and private properties. As a shared space, the new quarter is interwoven in the fabric, responding to the private interests and the individual and public expressions of the building and the city.

"Only an equal, fair and pleasant experience of space guarantees its public quality."

The categories of public and private, in spaces and even in life, are separated by tenuous lines. I imagine my city plan, in my daily life paths, designed in a Nolli-like manner. As La Pianta Grande di Roma[2] where the enclosed public spaces, such as the colonnades in St. Peter's Square or the Pantheon, are represented as open civic spaces. My obsession as an architect goes to the point that I would love to design every place that I can access, every public space—every street, every garden—and even design the private spaces that host collective functions, such as religious and trading places, churches and worship buildings, coffee shops, restaurants, museums, administration buildings, and everything else. Cities have a wealth of urban identity, and design provides such identity. The architect has the civic responsibility to contribute to such an endeavor, and beyond the totalitarian dream (or nightmare) of a continuous design and redesign, it lays the hope of enhancing our experience of space. Only an equal, fair and pleasant experience of space guarantees its public quality. Yes, architecture is politics.

1 Raquel Henriques da Silva, "Das Avenidas Novas à Avenida de Berna" in *Revista de História de Arte*, n. 2 (Lisbon, 2006), pp. 142–176.

2 See Giovanni Battista Nolli, *La Pianta Grande di Roma* (1736–1748). http://nolli.uoregon.edu/. Nolli's map consists of twelve exquisitely engraved copper plates that measure approximately six feet high and seven feet wide when combined (176 cm by 208 cm). The map includes almost eight square miles of the densely built city as well as the surrounding terrain. It also identifies nearly two thousand sites of cultural significance. Nolli's map is an extraordinary technical achievement that represents a milestone in the art and science of cartography. The map not only records the streets, squares and public urban places of Rome, but Nolli carefully renders hundreds of building interiors with detailed plans.

Breda
5th
25sep—
25okt 2015
GRAPHIC
DESIGN
FESTIVAL
BREDA

CHRIST & GANTENBEIN

Kunstmuseum Basel Extension

Christoph Gantenbein and Emanuel Christ

PROJECT NAME
Kunstmuseum Basel Extension

ARCHITECT/S
Christ & Gantenbein, Basel / CH

BUILDING PURPOSE
Museum

LOCATION
Basel, Switzerland

CONSTRUCTION PERIOD
2012–2016

BRICK TYPE
Clay blocks

BRICK AWARD CATEGORY
Sharing public spaces

BRICK 18 Grand Prize Winner

The Kunstmuseum Basel possesses one of the most eminent painting collections in the world. The 8,000-square-meter extension of the existing building, a listed structure erected in 1936, was opened in April 2016. Just a few steps from the Rhine, the Swiss architects Christ & Gantenbein erected a solitary gray structure that is connected through an underground hall below Dufourstraße with the main building.

On St.-Alban-Graben, the building jumps back a few meters like a monumental sculpture. The gesture is skillfully placed, since one would like to inevitably look upward and appreciate the work in its entirety after all. The façade consists of fired bricks, the red and yellow tones of which were extracted with nitrogen. The chemical process lets the building appear like a coarse-grained, black-and-white photograph in the middle of the city. One recognizes a gentle color gradient: While dark bricks were rather used in the street area, the material becomes successively brighter towards the top.

"Brick is an extremely versatile material," says architect Emanuel Christ. "It can be produced almost everywhere in the world, by hand or industrially, cheaply or also very expensively. Very few building materials offer such a large diversity." In the Kunstmuseum Basel addition, a conscious decision was made for a material that stands for timelessness, sustainability and structural precision: The entire outer shell of the façade gets by without a single expansion joint. "We wanted the new building to speak the same language as the existing structure with its mighty walls and distinctive horizontal stripes. At the same time, however, we wanted to tell a completely distinct, new story."

> "The architecture has something like an aura, like a soul, like a mental patina."

And that it does. At a height of twelve to fifteen meters, a large, slightly sublime stripe attracts attention on the main façades. At dusk the formal secret is lifted: LED lights are integrated in the relief-like grooves made of molded bricks that suddenly let the house speak through indirect lighting: One time it is an illuminated diamond or stripe ornament that hovers like a Burlington sweater over the façade; another time it is the trace of fluorescent letters that slowly wander around the frieze, giving information about the current exhibition or posing rhetorical questions to the city.

In the interior spaces as well, the architects seem to have removed the color. Gray Bardiglio marble from Cararra was laid in the stairwell and in the hallway; the walls above are covered with a likewise gray, rough scraped plaster. "This was exactly our intention," the architect explains. "It is almost as if someone had desaturated the picture in Photoshop up to monochromy. The color variety of the second half of the 20th century takes center stage."

Besides ongoing temporary exhibitions, works particularly by American artists since the 1960s—among them, Roy Lichtenstein, Andy Warhol, Jasper Johns, Mark Rothko, Frank Stella, Donald Judd and Cy Twombly—are to be displayed in the new exhibition spaces. "From the curating perspective, I can say that art and architecture harmonize well and that the spaces are wonderfully suited for working," Nina Zimmer, curator and assistant director of the museum, points out. "The architecture is indeed brand new, but it now already has something like an aura, like a soul, like a mental patina." The Kunstmuseum has thereby gained itself as a valuable exhibit.

Jury Statement

"The Kunstmuseum Basel is a very interesting and strong project in terms of its material investigation that it is powerful in the way it has employed brick work as the external expression of this big, new building. A public building and a national institution, it's a building that offers a kind of public accessibility appropriate for its program. Sharing public space is only part of the story though; the sharing extends to the city itself. It is not just about the interior spaces themselves, but also about the manner in which this very bold brick volume positions itself accurately within the immediate context that it sits. This project has provoked a widespread discussion within the architectural community. But it must be added, in terms of the purpose of this award, that this is a very fitting example of what is possible to do in contemporary terms with a building of such civil importance—the way that brick can feel noble and highly crafted."

The finest surfaces—also from up close

The warm, gray shade arose by treating the fired bricks with nitrogen.

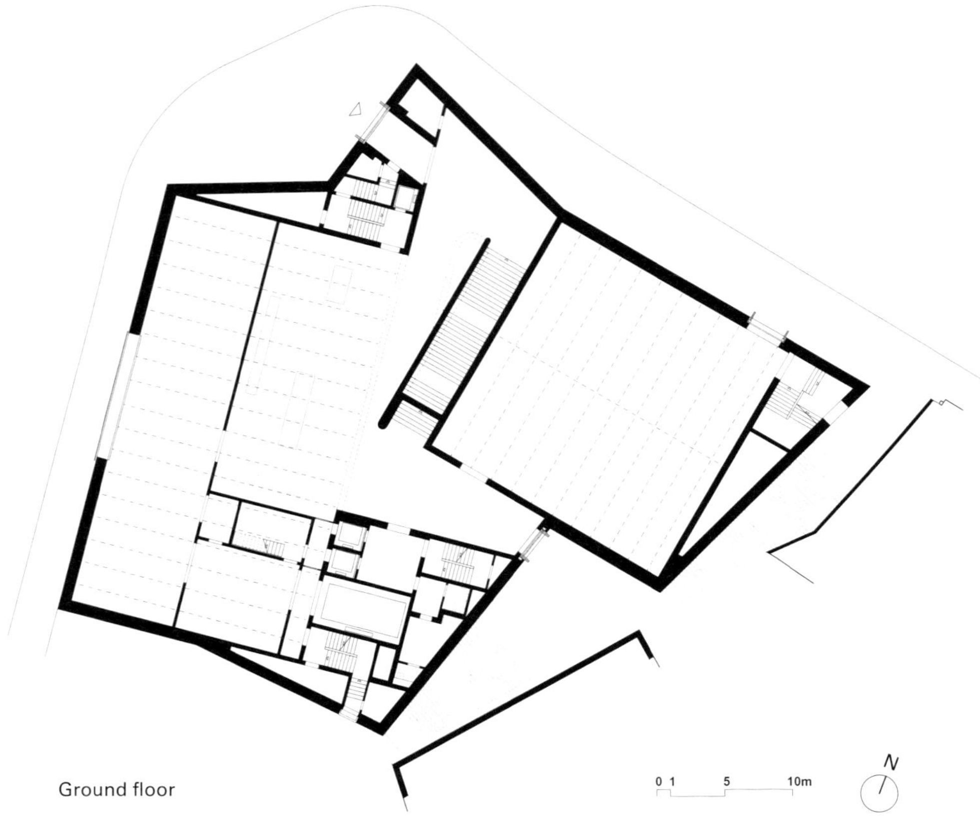

Ground floor

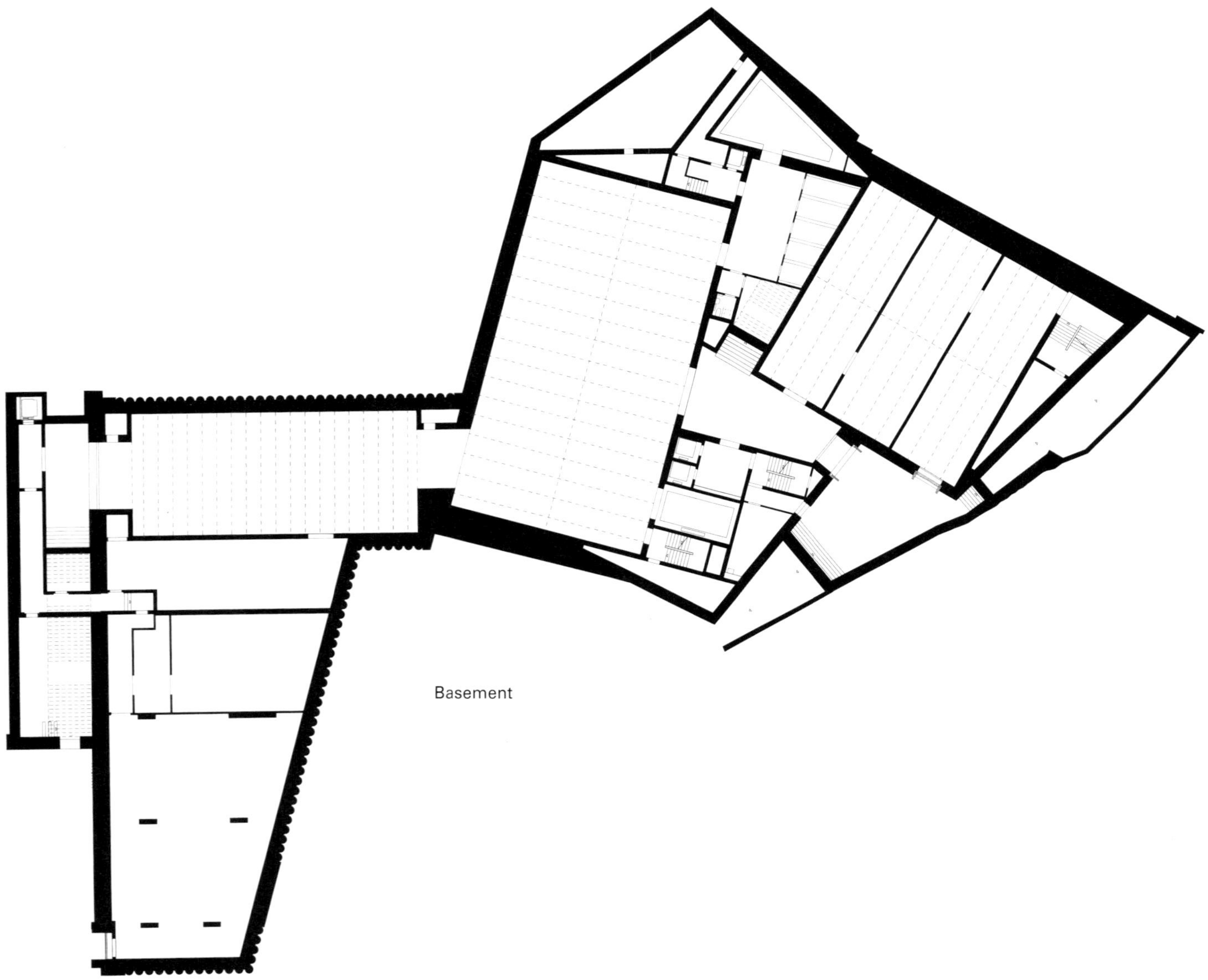

Basement

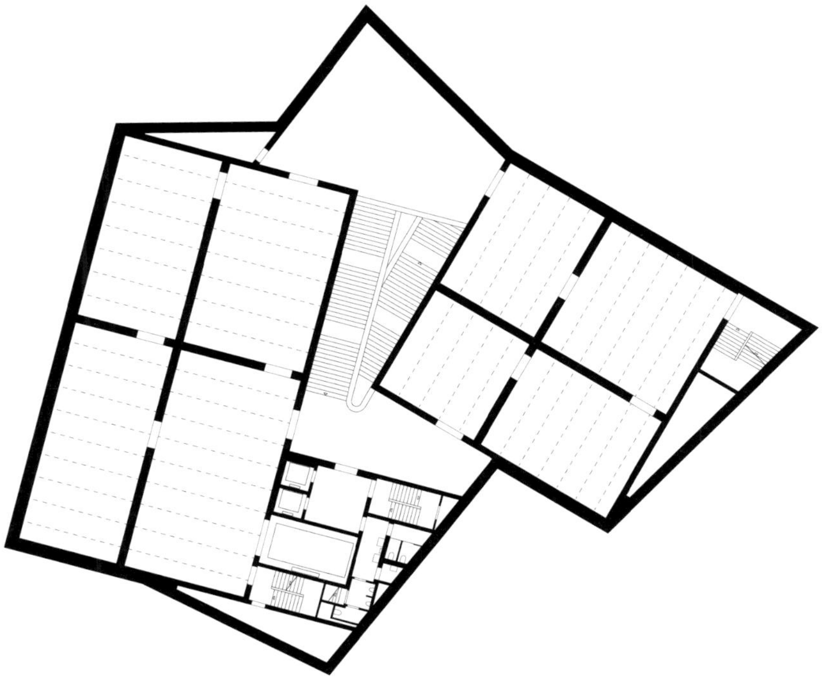

Second floor

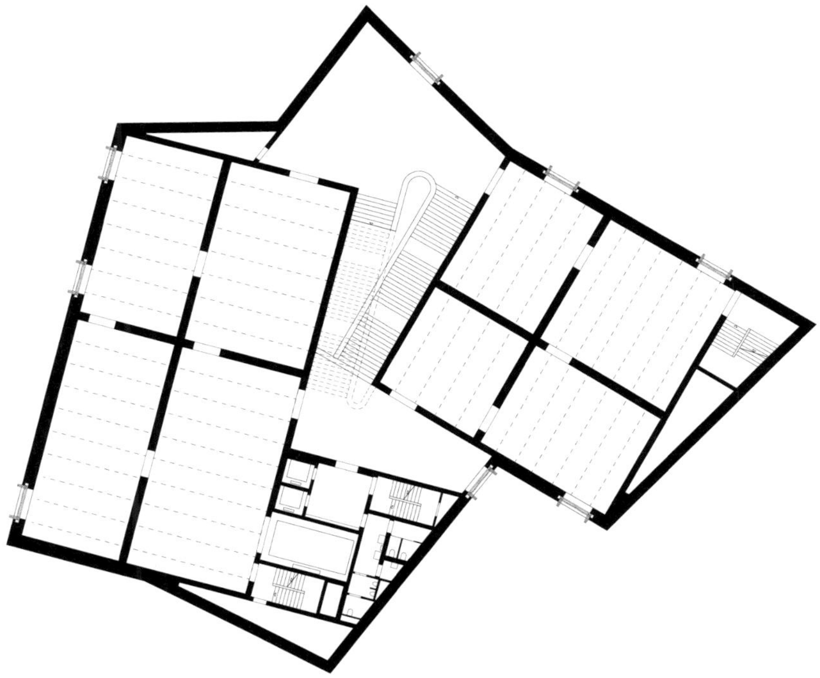

First floor

The distinctive solitary structure in an urban context

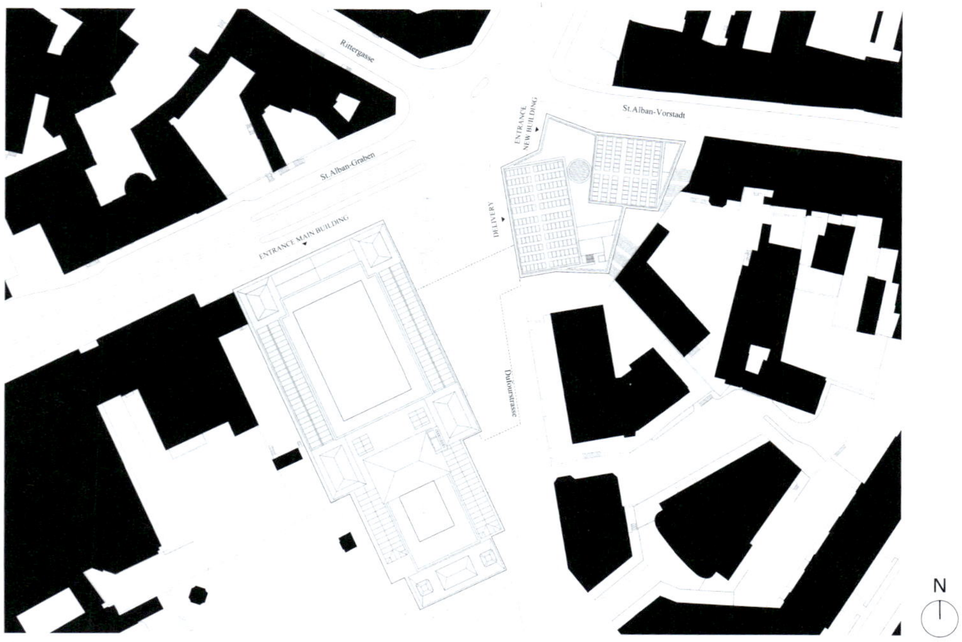

Site plan

LEDs that send messages out into the urban space are integrated into the dark stripe.

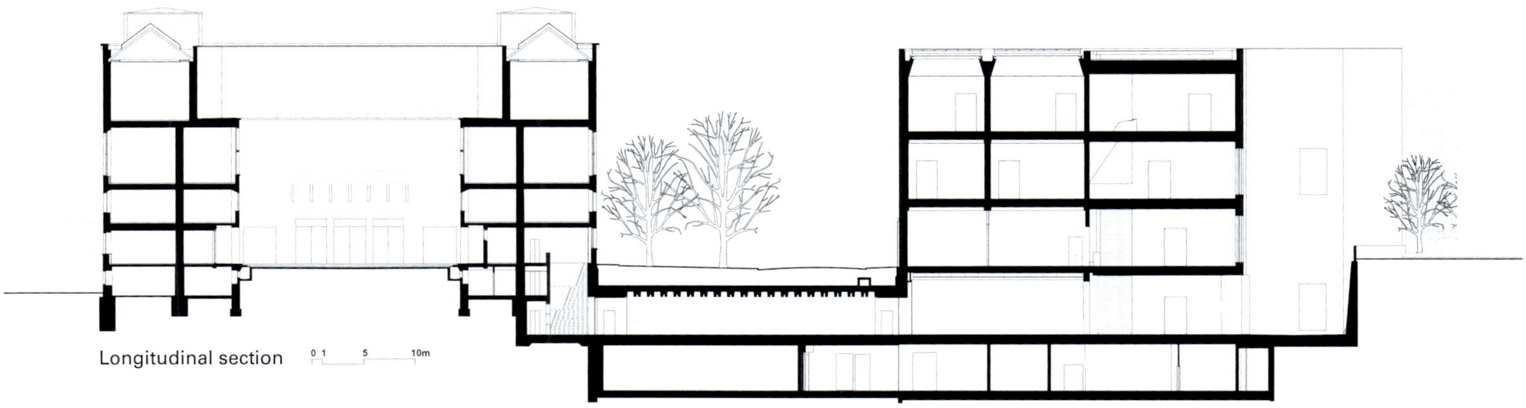

Longitudinal section 0 1 5 10m

NICOLÁS CAMPODONICO ESTUDIO

San Bernardo Chapel

Nicolás Esteban Campodonico

PROJECT NAME
San Bernardo Chapel

ARCHITECT/S
Nicolás Campodonico Estudio,
San Lorenzo / AR

BUILDING PURPOSE
Sacral building

LOCATION
La Playosa, Argentina

CONSTRUCTION PERIOD
2012–2015

BRICK TYPE
Clay blocks

BRICK AWARD CATEGORY
Sharing public spaces

BRICK 18 Special Prize Winner

This chapel is a small masterpiece. United in it are a sensitive dealing with the location, an imaginative engagement with the principle of church construction, an equally simple as well as diverse and impressive shape, and a concentrated reduction.

The chapel is dedicated to the patron saint of a small community near where it was erected. It stands where an old farmstead was situated, in the Argentine Pampa, framed by a small grove that shields it towards the east. Neither running water nor electricity is available at the site itself. Only the light of the sun and nature determine the atmosphere. Bordered by walls, the premises exude a cheerful, monastic mood.

One enters the area from the north; a surface paved with bricks is spread out in front of the chapel and bounded by a low bench, likewise of brick. One goes round the building on its eastern side before entering it from the southern side. A tapering path leads into the interior, guiding the visitor into the chapel, the impressive interior of which cannot be anticipated. Whereas the exterior is bordered by straight surfaces, the interior is characterized by curved ones. A half cylinder opening towards the west rises above the foundation walls and merges into a spherical segment to the east and concludes the chapel through a flat, open arch under which the interior is connected to the exterior. The sphere inscribed into the construction finds itself again as a projection in the brick flooring and is likewise traced by the gallery lying in the west. Bricks applied to the lower side of the gallery are also oriented to the middle point of the circle paraphrasing the sphere.

This space, constructed with traditional craftsmanship, is already impressive enough. Yet what significantly enhances it is how the architect deals with light which, as a metaphor of divine truth, plays such an essential role for Christianity. The aperture that opens to the west captures the light of the sun that one can see wandering along the wall. The shape is conceived so that light does not strike any protrusions or edges. Two wooden poles are arranged on the gallery, one vertically, the other horizontally. They are not connected to each other. First the course of the sun, which projects the shadows of the two wooden poles as lines on the interior surface of the chapel, gradually brings these shadow lines together and lets them ultimately appear in the east as a cross. For the architect this is the symbolization and visualization of the way Jesus went. The side of the altar in churches, traditionally facing the east, the sunrise and the origin of light, is clearly and manifestly translated into a contemporary form. The fact that the building material of brick, which is traditional for the region, was exclusively used underscores this meditative clarity that transcends the course of time and the light falling from the west.

> "In the plains there are no stones or woods, just earth. The brick is the Pampa's 'natural' material, so it is the only material used."

The old bricks of the house that previously stood there were used for the outer walls. Their patina ensures that the site, the building and nature combine into an entity. In the evening, the warm light shines out from the flat arch of the east side from the inside to the outside, and thus conveys, in a once-again distinctive manner, what has culminated on the inside in the evening in the fusion of both lines into a cross.

Sharing public spaces

Jury Statement

"A traditional project—not only in the use of material, but also in the configuration of space. The most interesting aspect of this project is that the outside doesn't reveal the interior space. A very poetic and special project because it is full of surprises and will never become outdated. It is done as an extraordinary craft. Old bricks have been re-utilized and the structure of the brick wall uses light in a completely interesting way. It is a small project and that is the great thing about it, since it creates so many emotions and so much awe as you go inside. It is powerful with a very small configuration, but there is a lot of skill, sensibility and feeling towards light and the material of brick. It is sure it is a place of great joy for anyone who goes there and it was a great joy for us to review it."

An entity of nature, construction and materiality

The east side of the chapel with the bench in the foreground

Old bricks were used for the external walls and the wall around the chapel.

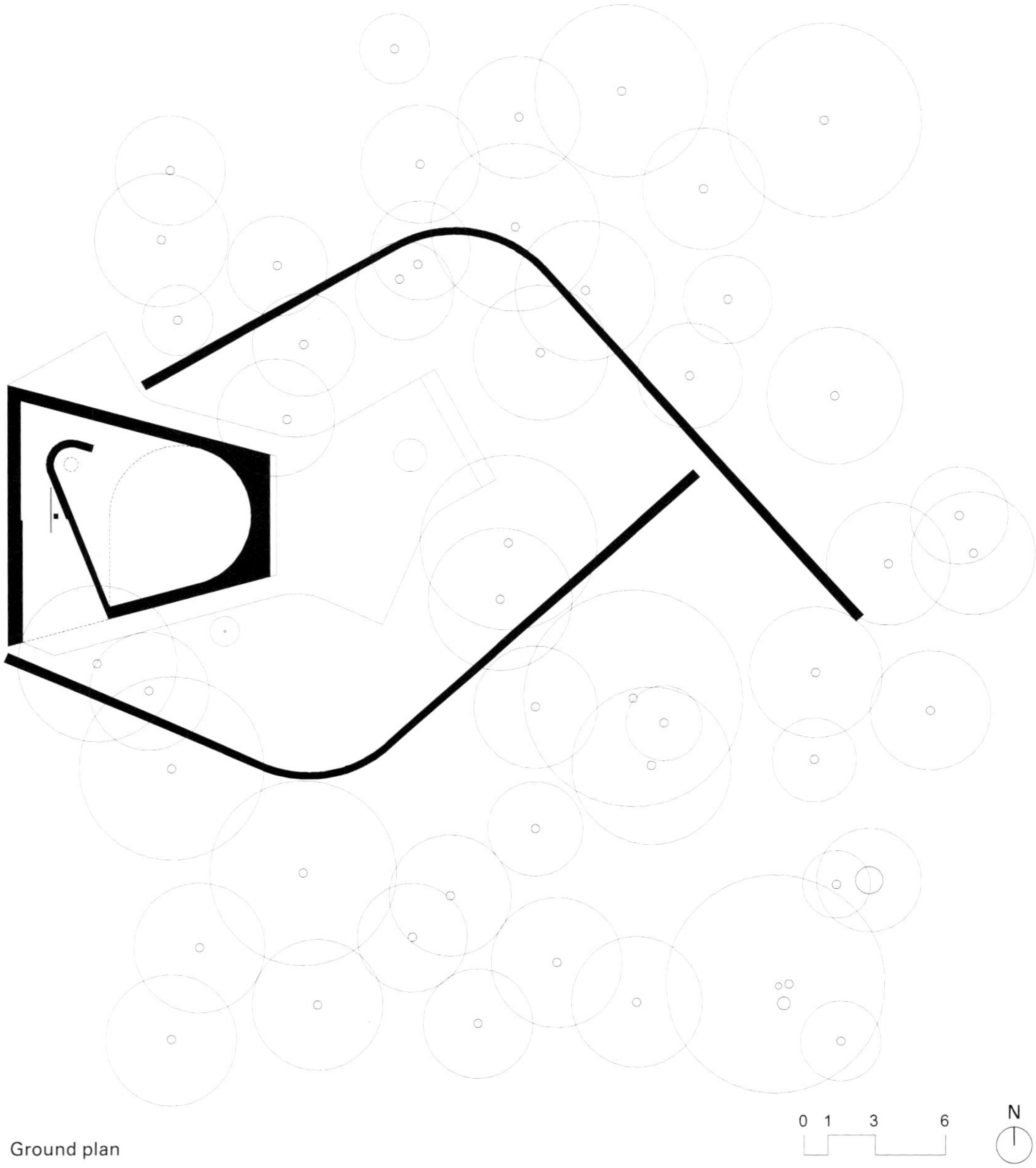

Ground plan

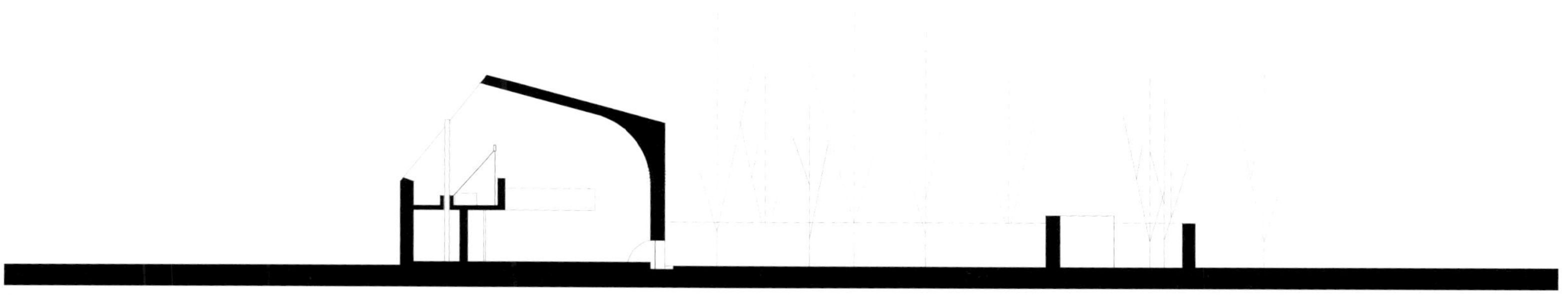

Longitudinal section

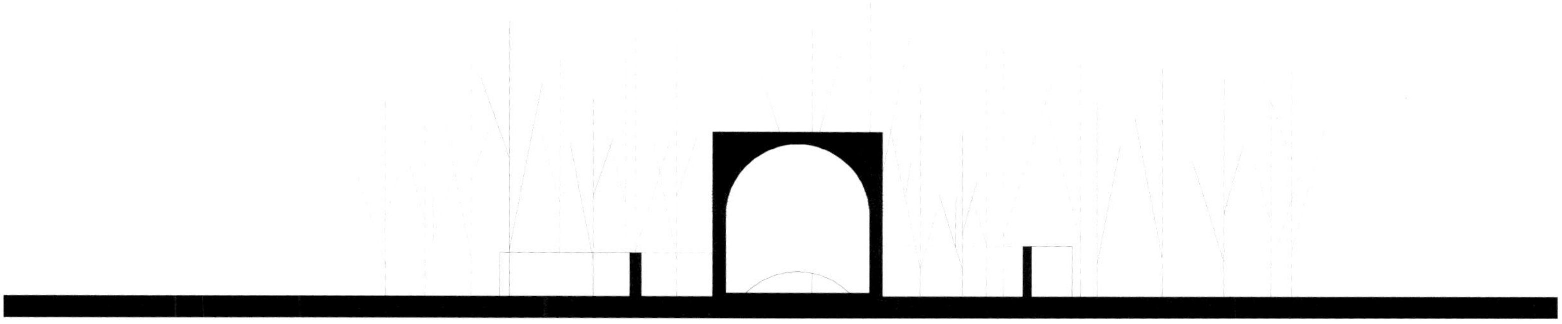

Cross section

Russian Monastery Church St. Georg

Sergei Tchoban

PROJECT NAME
Russian Monastery Church St. Georg

ARCHITECT/S
Tchoban Voss Architekten, Berlin / DE

BUILDING PURPOSE
Sacral building

LOCATION
Götschendorf, Germany

CONSTRUCTION PERIOD
2012–2017

BRICK TYPE
Facing bricks

BRICK AWARD CATEGORY
Sharing public spaces

Götschendorf is located in the middle of Uckermark, a moraine landscape in the solitude of Brandenburg. Surrounded by forest edges and small farmhouses, a Russian Orthodox church suddenly and surprisingly emerges on the side of the road. The plain, white structure is part of an Orthodox monastery complex founded by the former journalist and news correspondent Norbert Kuchinke in 2006 after he had given up his job in Moscow and decided to devote his life from this time on to the less worldly things.

"Planning a new church is already a special building task in itself."

A square space measuring seventeen meters in side width and ten meters in height forms the basis of this sacral building without a plinth. In the altar area, the ground plan is extended by three semicircular apses. Providing room for up to 200 people, the space is completed according to Russian-Byzantine architectural tradition by a cross-in-square cupola with a round lantern and onion dome. The distinctive spire soars 26 meters into the sky.

The materials used here appear unusually reduced: The entire façade is clad with bright, hand-molded bricks, which were subsequently covered with white slurry. Behind the subtle cement veil, the ochre, gray, and red tones of the fired material shimmer through. Depending on the incidence of light, the surface seems to glitter from silvery to copper-toned as a result. Together with the sculpturally formed doorway arches, window surrounds, vertical pilaster strips and the clearly pronounced mortar joints, a subtle depth arises in this manner, instilling a certain liveliness in the midst of calm. A wooden eaves cornice and bright gray-weathered roof shingles made of wood conclude the structure.

"Planning a new church is already a special building task in itself," says Sergei Tchoban. "But in this case, the additional challenge entailed inscribing a Russian Orthodox church building into a Protestant-shaped town." Born and raised in St. Petersburg, the architect has a foible for subtlety and sensitivity up to the last detail, and already caused an unexcited stir with his Museum for Architectural Drawing on Prenzlauer Berg in Berlin, which he erected in 2013. "I therefore decided to reduce and to abstract the appearance compared to classic Orthodox churches and to fit the building harmonically into its setting."

The result is a simple sacred building with few accents. It unmistakably bears witness to its spiritual origin, colors and materials, but adapts very unpretentiously to the conditions on site. Erected in such a way, the essence of a Russian Orthodox church is an innovative, because unorthodox contribution to contemporary sacral architecture. In the coming years the monastery church is to be expanded by a guest house for pilgrims and visitors.

Monastery church based on the Russian-Byzantine building tradition

Sharing public spaces

Hand-molded bricks covered with white slurry allow the original color of the bricks to shimmer through.

Activity and Dance Center

Mathieu Berteloot and Heleen Hart

PROJECT NAME
Activity and Dance Center

ARCHITECT/S
HBAAT – Hart Berteloot Atelier Architecture Territoir, Lille/FR

BUILDING PURPOSE
Leisure center

LOCATION
Quesnoy-sur-Deûle, France

CONSTRUCTION PERIOD
2014–2015

BRICK TYPE
Facing bricks

BRICK AWARD CATEGORY
Sharing public spaces

Quesnoy-sur-Deûle is a small community at the northernmost tip of France. The proximity to Lille, Calais and the Belgian border has brought the town a brisk amount of through-traffic since antiquity. Even today, around 18,000 ships travel the Deûle annually. Barely 70 meters from this strategically so important river, where a run-down kayak club once characterized the location, a minimalist gem is to be found. HBAAT erected a small dance and movement center here for the youngest members of society. The Dance and Activity Center, part of the cultural and educational program of the Lille Region, became operative in June 2015.

"We see ourselves not only as architects, but also as companions and project developers," say Heleen Hart and Mathieu Berteloot, who run their office in Lille and are specialized, among other things, in public facilities such as day care centers, schools, libraries and cultural buildings. "Therefore, we also supervised this project from the very beginning—from the first meetings with the community, to the analysis of local conditions, to the planning and construction."

In order to be able to take maximum advantage of the somewhat more than 1,000-square-meter-large lot, which is surrounded by streets, single-family houses and a school, the architects decided to shift the structure to the northern edge and to locate a narrow, but well-utilizable open space on the southern part. The small, sealed inner courtyard is enclosed on all sides by a cement wall. Greenery was consciously left out. Everything here is influenced by the physical, space-spanning movement between the inside and the outside.

"We see ourselves not only as architects, but also as companions and project developers."

The façade is made of exposed concrete and white clinkers. As mostly found in industrial buildings, these were bricked in an offset stretcher bond. The gray joints allow the raw, industrial visual effect to clearly stand out. Surface refinements like plaster or color are sought in vain. On one hand, the project had to be erected in a very cost-conscious manner; on the other hand, the color here is reserved for the dancing boys and girls. During performances, the house and inner courtyard mutate into a minimalist, nearly dematerialized picture-frame stage.

Clarity and simplicity also dominate the interior. Besides the three instruction rooms, which completely open up towards the courtyard through wall-to-ceiling sliding glass doors, there are wardrobes, sanitary facilities as well as a 170-square-meter-large dance and ballet hall. Among the materials used are plastic floors, locally produced, ready-made concrete bricks, as well as unvarnished pine plywood for sliding doors and wall cladding. The bricolage made of cheap and recycled construction materials blends in perfectly with the surroundings dedicated to learning, dancing and the childish love of adventure.

Exposed concrete and white clinkers with gray joints on the façade

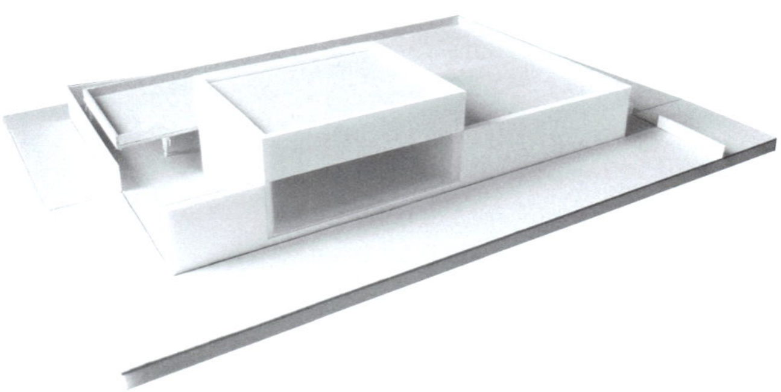

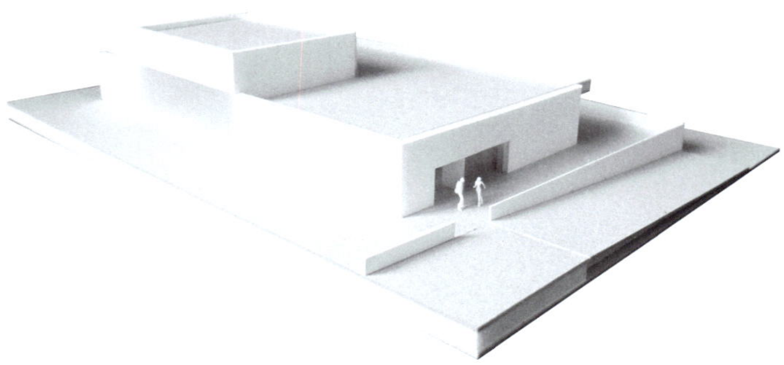

Model photos

The house and courtyard are kept in a neutral gray; the color comes from the children and the furnishings.

The materialization underscores the industrial character.

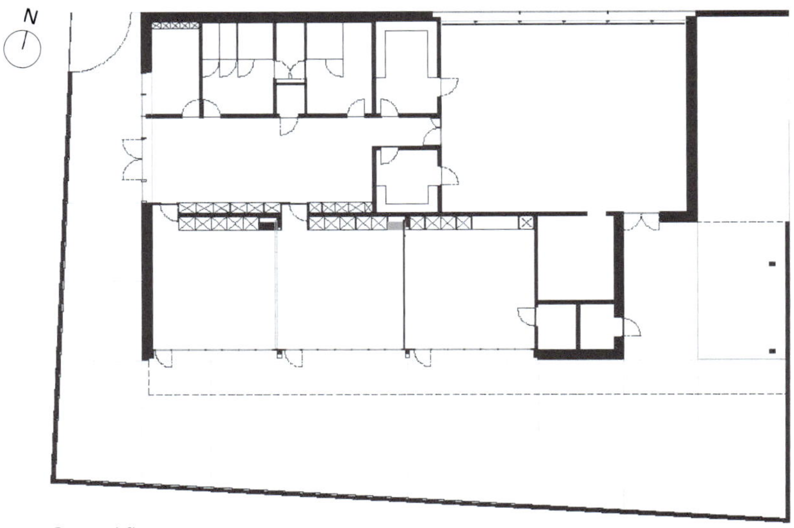

Ground floor

SEA – STUDIO FOR ENVIRONMENT AND ARCHITECTURE

The Temple and the People

Venu Kopal, Shyam Kumar and Hari Krishna Karri

PROJECT NAME
The Temple and the People

ARCHITECT/S
SEA – Studio for Environment and Architecture, Hyderabad / IN

BUILDING PURPOSE
Sacral building

LOCATION
Vennached, India

CONSTRUCTION PERIOD
2014–2015

BRICK TYPE
Clay blocks

BRICK AWARD CATEGORY
Sharing public spaces

Indian architecture is considered as one of the world's oldest. Its beginnings lie in the cities of the early Indus culture in the third century BC. Since the seventh century AD, that building typology known up to this day as Hindu Temple, respectively Mandir, has been practiced. The design, sequence of rooms and ornamentation follow strict rules that differ from region to region.
In Vennached, a small village southwest of the metropolis of Hyderabad, this new temple, which breaks with all traditions of Hindu construction—at least at first glance—was erected.

> "Through the once symmetrically incidental, another time unpredictably dancing sunlight on the structural brick surface, the light itself becomes the ornament."

The architect Hari Krishna Karri planned a plain temple dedicated to the saint Shirdi Sai Baba and was to be constructed in locally common Tandur stone.
In consultation with the clients and the authorities, however, the decision was made to switch from the gray stone to a more robust building material. Since it performed better in tests in regard to sturdiness, building logistics and durability, the choice fell to brick. The deployment of material is innovative and unique in this way.

Perforated clay bricks with a material thickness of 15 centimeters were used on the walls and outer walls of the temple room. For the seven-meter-high shikhara, as the convexly stepped tower is called, ten-centimeter-thick bricks were used. The characteristic slant of the bricks, which result in several sequences of slats, is a reinterpretation of the tracery-like perforated screens, the so-called jali, which are traditionally found in Indian architecture.

"In retrospect, I am very happy about this development," mentions the architect Karri, who describes himself as an agnostic and made his first foray into sacred architecture with the temple, "since in combination with the concrete, the grout, the omnipresent Tandur gray of the surrounding buildings and the deep blue of the sky, wonderful, warm contrasts, which we would have otherwise had to do without, emerged." A Srivathsan, architecture theoretician and Academic Director of the CEPT University in Ahmedabad, describes the choice of material in one of his texts as eminently harmonious, because the red not only reflects the earth, but also the different saffron tones that are to be found in many Hindu buildings and objects.

"But the most important element of every temple," says the architect, "is the ornamentation that usually shows people, animals and deities in all conceivable colors. In this temple, however, the resplendent decoration is abstracted in the pure geometry of the shikhara. Through the once symmetrically incidental, another time unpredictably dancing sunlight on the structural brick surface, the light itself becomes the ornament. And the color ... it comes from the people who go in and out of here." One understands now at the latest why the architect describes his sacral debut project as a distillate, as the absolute essence of a traditional Hindu temple.

The slant of the bricks draws upon the tradition of tracery-like perforated screens.

St. Olav's Catholic Cathedral

Eggen Arkitekter

PROJECT NAME
St. Olav's Catholic Cathedral

ARCHITECT/S
Eggen Arkitekter, Trondheim, NO

BUILDING PURPOSE
Sacral building

LOCATION
Trondheim, Norway

CONSTRUCTION PERIOD
2015–2016

BRICK TYPE
Facing bricks

BRICK AWARD CATEGORY
Sharing public spaces

With around 200,000 inhabitants, Trondheim is Norway's third largest city after Oslo and Bergen. The Roman Catholic community is traditionally very small, but through the strong influx from Eastern and Southeastern European countries it has vigorously grown in the past years. "The old church was much too small for our needs," recalls Egil Mogstad, pastor of the newly erected St. Olav's Cathedral. "Besides, there were construction flaws and symptoms of old age like mold and corrosion. There was an urgent need for action."

> "For us, the brick and the classic architectural elements are an intellectual connection to the rich history of this city."

In the year 2010, a national architecture competition for a new cathedral was tendered. Unobtrusive and classical-appearing, the winning project is comprised of a three-aisled basilica with a freestanding church tower and diverse annexes where the parish center, library and three priest's apartments are situated. Bright, gray-brown brick is the dominating building material.

"The location in Trondheim is unique," the architects explain, "St. Olav's Cathedral lies on a prominent bottleneck at the south end of the historic old city, on the bank of the Nidelva River, directly next to the Elgeseter Bridge and in the middle of beautiful art nouveau mansions. For this reason we decided to design the project in a very classical manner. We see the church as a modern interpretation of a traditional basilica."

The first impression is characterized by tenderness and elegance. Barely has the heavy oak door with its shimmering copper fittings closed when a warm, cozy interior space, holding up to 450 persons, opens up. It almost seems as if it had already been there forever. The main aisle, the side aisles and the pillars are homogenously kept in brick. A few Nordic-cool light beams fall into the space through the twelve windows in the clerestory. The altar is found in the round apse. A lightweight wooden roof structure with iron tension rods hovers above everything.

"For us, the brick and the classic architectural elements are an intellectual connection to the rich history of this city," both architects stress. "The plain construction with its changing brick surfaces lends the space calm, on the one hand, and a rich, vibrant relief texture, on the other hand. And, naturally, the mix of materials with the copper, the oak wood and the heavy, brushed limestone on the floor and on the altar is also an expression of authenticity and durability." In any case, the pastor of the sacral building is satisfied. During the consecration in November 2016, Egil Mogstad attested a prominently referencing, early Christian aesthetic to his cathedral: "This church is as beautiful as Santa Sabina in Rome, yet as modern as the 21st century deserves."

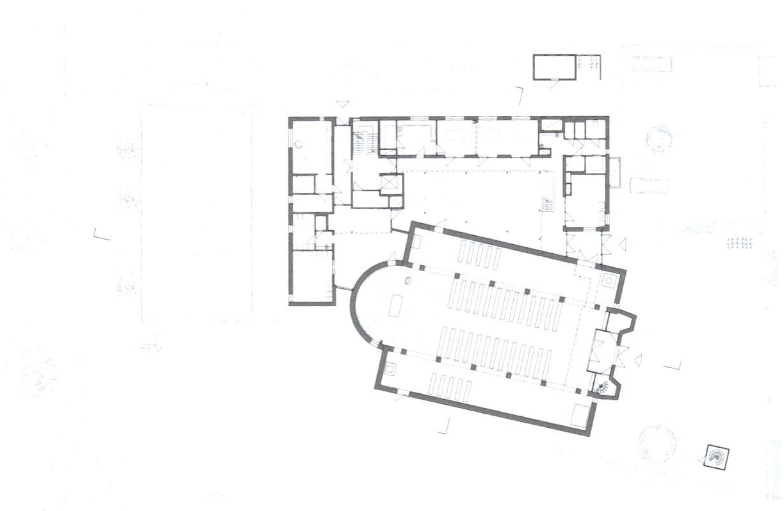

Ground plan

The use of brick, stone, wood and copper stands for authenticity and durability.

ANDREAS HELLER ARCHITECTS & DESIGNERS

European Hansemuseum Lübeck

Andreas Heller

PROJECT NAME
European Hansemuseum Lübeck

ARCHITECT/S
Andreas Heller Architects & Designers, Hamburg / DE

BUILDING PURPOSE
Museum

LOCATION
Lübeck, Germany

CONSTRUCTION PERIOD
2013–2015

BRICK TYPE
Facing bricks
Roof tiles
Paving bricks

BRICK AWARD CATEGORY
Sharing public spaces

In the history of the Hanseatic League, Lübeck plays a crucial role. It is no coincidence, therefore, that the largest Hansa museum in Europe came into being in 2015 in Lübeck.

> "With the architecture of the new museum building we have combined hand-crafted, high-quality brick materiality with elegant modernity."

Located on the northern edge of the inner city, the museum consists of a new structure and the renovated and restored buildings of the Castle Friary, one of the most important medieval monastery complexes in Northern Germany. Through the restoration, its eventful history has been made comprehensible and integrated into the over 7,000-square-meter-large compound. Prior to that, additions and installations not worthy of preserving had been removed. With few amendments, decidedly identifiable as those of a new era through the use of white concrete or bronze as materials, the architect clarifies the overall spatial situation and shapes it into an entity.
The new, two-story building snuggles up to the slope of the hill upon which the Castle Friary rises, thereby bordering the old city towards the Trave River and the port facilities. In the typical local material of a red clinker, the closed front of the museum appears at this spot like a reminiscence of the city wall that once stood here. About in its middle, a public staircase leads up the Castle Friary hill to a roof terrace, an observation platform, and further on into the old city.

> "In the interplay of the new structure with the listed monument of the Castle Friary and the outdoor facilities, the European Hansemuseum has melded into a distinctive sign that forges a link between the past and the present."

A new brick, based on the format of traditional Brick Gothic which spread throughout the entire Baltic region with the Hansa, was developed for the façade. Hand-pressed in wooden molds, the bricks were coated with different slurries that result in various color shades; the darker bricks were used mostly higher up in the façade. In addition, the joints were recessed towards the top, so that the ensuing shadowing increases the effect of the darker brick even more. The overall result, therefore, is a richly varied picture that splendidly complements the historic surroundings and the old Friary buildings.

At the southern edge, the modern shape of the new building segues into a traditional gabled house, which is adorned with an ornamental façade made of quatrefoil motifs likewise based on Brick Gothic and found again, for instance, on the windows of the Friary. Also hand-produced, the bricks on this façade feature a rough and vibrant surface.

The museum is accessed from the stairs leading through the building, which, in addition to information about the Hansa and spatial installations that take viewers back into the era of the Hansa, displays original documents and archaeological finds. Moreover, the building now surrounds a former excavation site. In this way the museum makes history accessible at many levels: in the exhibits, in the historical and new sections of the complex, and in its architectural language.

A brick whose color shades vary on account of various slurries was developed for the façade.

The color gradient of the bricks gets darker going upwards while the joints get deeper.

The new building stands on the location of the former city wall.

PETER BÖHM ARCHITEKTEN

Philosophikum am Domplatz

Peter Böhm

PROJECT NAME
Philosophikum am Domplatz

ARCHITECT/S
Peter Böhm Architekten, Köln / DE

BUILDING PURPOSE
Education

LOCATION
Münster, Germany

CONSTRUCTION PERIOD
2011–2017

BRICK TYPE
Facing bricks

BRICK AWARD CATEGORY
Sharing public spaces

Home to the university philosophy department, the Philosophikum lies directly on the western edge of the central Domplatz (Cathedral Square) in the Westphalian city of Münster. Since the postwar era it has been located in an old building erected in 1903 as a seminary, which underwent major changes through additions and conversions following war damage. A modernization had become inevitable; moreover, the outdoor space on the sloping property was unsatisfactorily designed and an extension of the spatial offer desired. The Cologne-based office of Peter Böhm Architekten prevailed in a 2010 competition with a design that was completed in 2017.

After the additions were torn down, a long, narrow block was placed in front of the existing building. Five stories high, it is somewhat lower than the old building, since it adopts the eaves heights of the development bordering to the south. Because the new structure was additionally placed parallel to this development opposite it, an interstice that widens towards the old building and takes in the foyer as a glass hall resulted. Slightly stepped, the courtyard comfortably leads downwards from the Cathedral Square to the entrance at the western end of the new building. As a public space accessible to everyone, it also establishes a connection to a small park and a creek.

The façade is designed so that the old and the new become an entity. A sandstone façade covers the head of the old building; its section extending downwards is brightly plastered. For this reason the architects decided for a brick façade coated with yellowish, ochre-toned slurry, which orients itself in terms of color to the existing building. But the red of the brick, which is a frequently applied façade material here in Münster, nonetheless shimmers through. Clad in brick, the story-high pillars form a type of large shelf with the horizontal concrete elements, which reveal the stories. This thereby points to the fact that the new edifice's approximately 1,800 m²-large floor space is mainly used as a library. The pillars are arranged in front of the head end of the bookshelves: the inner spatial rhythm therefore structures the façade as well.

"The new building forms an entity with the old one, connected by a glass hall as an interstice. This uniform character is also strengthened by the materiality of the façades of brickwork, which are washed with a bright sand-colored lime-cement mortar. The reddish brick will glimmer only very slightly through this surface."

The dialog between old and new is to be experienced in the interior, too, where the carefully detailed brick walls of the new structure face the former outer façade of the old building. Situated in the modernized existing structure are lecture halls, offices, seminar and meeting rooms (as well as other departments) and—like before—an auditorium and a studio stage of the German Studies Institute. Thanks to the use of geothermal energy and the activation of the concrete slabs for heating and cooling, it is possible to utilize distance heating solely to cover the peak load and to otherwise fall back on renewable energy for the most part.

The university received a successfully renovated and attractively expanded building. Aside from that, the citizens of the municipality profit from an upgraded public space.

Red bricks were coated in yellowish ochre slurry.

View from the foyer to the lecture hall

BEZ + KOCK ARCHITEKTEN

Anneliese Brost Music Forum Ruhr

Martin Bez and Thorsten Kock

PROJECT NAME
Anneliese Brost Music Forum Ruhr

ARCHITECT/S
Bez + Kock Architekten, Stuttgart / DE

BUILDING PURPOSE
Concert hall

LOCATION
Bochum, Germany

CONSTRUCTION PERIOD
2013–2016

BRICK TYPE
Facing bricks

BRICK AWARD CATEGORY
Sharing public spaces

Erected from 1868 to 1872 in a neo-Gothic style, the St.-Marien-Kirche (St. Mary's Church) marks the beginning of the Bochum inner city expansion westwards. After a structural reform of the responsible diocese, the church was secularized in 2000 and was to be demolished; thanks to the commitment of citizens, art historians and the conductor of the Bochum Symphony Orchestra, Steven Sloane, it was finally able to be preserved as a part of the Anneliese Brost Music Forum Ruhr.

Seating somewhat more than 900 listeners, the concert hall of the Bochum Symphony Orchestra, which they had long been missing up to then, connects to the sides of the church widthwise in the nave towards the south. A flexibly programmable multifunctional hall was added in the north. Owing to the single-story transition area between the church and the halls, the old building distinctly makes an appearance in keeping with its original function. The side rooms of the concert hall are also set apart by such an interstice, elegantly and manifestly dividing the large total volume in this manner.

The façades of the new structures are made of bright, lime-washed, terracotta-red bricks which were specially produced for this building assignment. They display the new without completely distancing themselves from the old: St. Mary's Church had also been built of brick, the typical local building material. Placed in a precise and concentrated fashion in the largely closed façade, the new doors and window frames blend excellently into this dialog of old and new.

"This is a model example of successful and mutually fruitful collaboration between the client, planner and architect. It was the only possible way to further develop the architect's spatial ideas with good acoustics and the client's wishes into a space valued by everyone."

The foyer of the new music center, which can be accessed via the freestanding chancel, now forms the interior of St. Mary's Church. Like the chancel, the tower porch in the west also emerges out of the alignment of the entire complex. After secularization, the church interior had considerably suffered—now it has been newly staged in a vibrant white. On the inside, the view to the brick façade of the old building is possible on its west side, as well as in the entrance areas of the concert halls. The new bricks can also be found again on the walls there, varying the correspondence between the existing building and the extension a second time.

In the concert hall itself, the seats are arranged so that the orchestra is surrounded by the audience and a close atmosphere of shared experience is created. Made of cherry, the wall panels lend warmth to the space. Meshed grating on the ceiling and behind the podium, as well as slight curvatures on the front side of the hall may recall the interior of a nave and thus establish a reference to the church on this symbolic level, too. But whoever does not share this association will appreciate that the church was not torn down and has meanwhile become a center of cultural life in a new way.

Like the former church, the Musikforum also features a brick façade.

Passage into the concert hall

The old bricks are preserved.

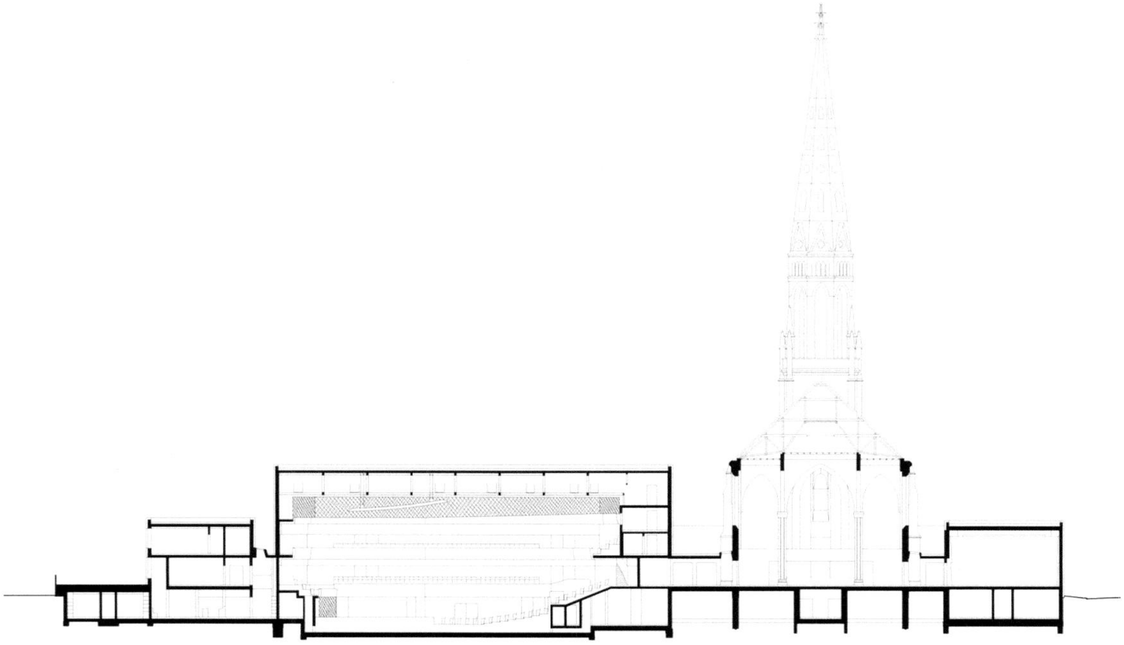

Longitudinal section

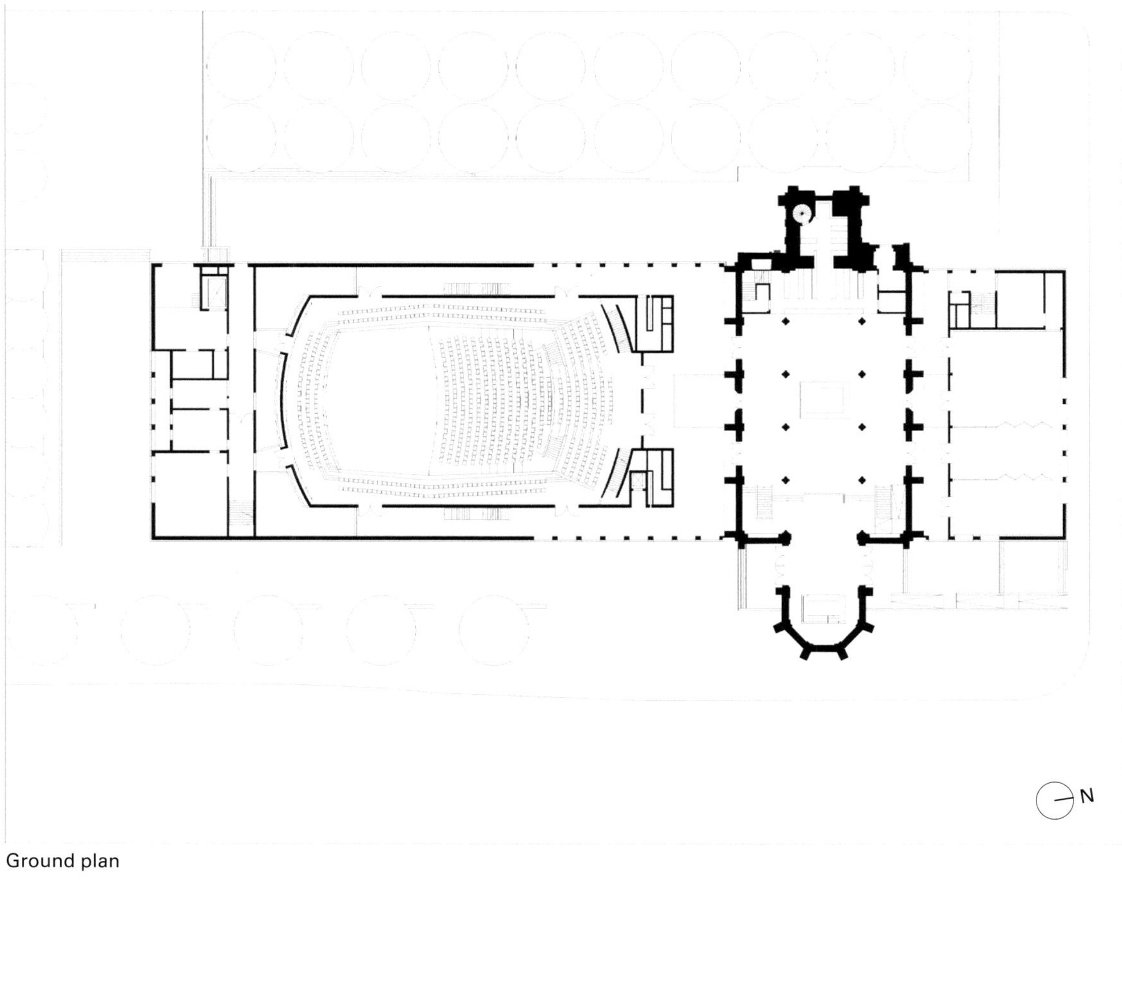

Ground plan

LUNDGAARD & TRANBERG ARKITEKTER

Kannikegården

Lundgaard & Tranberg Arkitekter

PROJECT NAME
Kannikegården

ARCHITECT/S
Lundgaard & Tranberg Arkitekter, Copenhagen / DK

BUILDING PURPOSE
Offices / multipurpose hall

LOCATION
Ribe, Denmark

CONSTRUCTION PERIOD
2014–2015

BRICK TYPE
Facing bricks
Paving bricks

BRICK AWARD CATEGORY
Sharing public spaces

Ribe, once an important place of trade on the North Sea coast, is Denmark's oldest city and a bishop's see since the 14th century. The cathedral is the center of the well-preserved medieval city and one of the most important sights. Sensibly fit into the neighborhood, a new building for the parish council and the cathedral staff, which includes a public auditorium, was completed in 2015 right across from it.

During construction work, the crew came upon remnants of the cathedral courtyard wall dating from the 12th century. In order to preserve and make them accessible, the architects split the building into two parts: In the lower part, glazed on all sides and bordered by rough, exposed concrete walls, the uncovered archaeological findings can be viewed. Rough wooden slats structure the façade. Since the historical site lies deeper than the present-day ground level, a terraced open space was laid out as a small atrium, in order to afford good natural lighting. Steel steps with an industrial look and feel lead from a small foyer and a gangway down to the old ruins. Everything here has been kept unwrought and original.

Resting upon concrete pillars above this ground floor, the actual new building with offices, the meeting room and the event space is elevated. A sweeping, far drawn down roof with a narrow base is pulled over the glazed ground floor like a bonnet. As a consequence, the slope of the roof already begins on the first floor. The window openings are irregular and, as required, nonetheless quite sparingly arranged so that the character of the closed volume dominates and the contrast between the open lower and closed upper part is not impaired.

> "The upper part of the building is covered with specially developed façade tiles in reddish brown shades comparable to the city's and the region's characteristic, brick houses – but as a more contemporary interpretation due to the larger size of the tiles."

The steel frame construction of the upper floors is completely clad with brick tiles. Adapted to the surroundings, the façade cladding consists of hand-produced, five-centimeter-thick plates with a surface of 63 × 35 centimeters, which are mounted on top of each other in an imbricated manner on a lattice construction. This brick tile format was specifically developed for this building. Rather undemanding, the mounting technique follows a centuries-old tradition, ensuring that the individual tiles can be easily replaced. The roof gutter on the lower edge is likewise clad with brick tiles; it protrudes slightly, thereby setting the upper stories apart from the glazed basement.

Through the directed control of the oxygen feed during the firing, the bricks received exactly the range of color tones with which they blend into the surroundings and incorporate the rust-red hues of the neighboring buildings. Production traces and surface irregularities were consciously taken into account in order to not let the new building appear as a foreign body within its historic setting. In this way, the historic center of the old city was properly and worthily enriched with this new building.

The brick plates cover the entire structure of the upper floors.

The coloring of the bricks corresponds to that of the surrounding historical buildings.

Terraced open space on the south side

The wall remnants of the old cathedral courtyard

Kopfholz School

Roger Boltshauser

PROJECT NAME
Kopfholz School

ARCHITECT/S
Boltshauser Architekten, Zurich / CH

BUILDING PURPOSE
Education

LOCATION
Adliswil, Switzerland

CONSTRUCTION PERIOD
2013–2014

BRICK TYPE
Facing bricks

BRICK AWARD CATEGORY
Sharing public spaces

The Kopfholz School building is a substantial extension to an existing school ensemble from the early 1970s in Adliswil, a small village on the south side of Lake Zurich. The new building, designed by Roger Boltshauser, is situated north of the existing sports hall amid the green surroundings composed of mature trees. Over four floors and an underground, the new building accommodates a large variety of functions such as kindergarten rooms on the lower floors, schoolrooms and a music room on the higher floors, with additional offices and therapy rooms that function as an extension to the school. The floor plans are organized around a compact core with stairs. An articulated window for each classroom faces one direction and a window in the support room faces a different direction to enhance the play of light within the building. The windows are arranged and shifted over two floors to scale down the building. Almost cubic, the volume has slightly shifted façades which furthermore support the pavilion typology of the school extension.

The façades of the new schoolhouse are constructed as massive walls. The material palette with warm gray window frames and nuanced brick carefully fits the new building into its green environs. The large closed surfaces of the building are clad in bricks that are cast into prefabricated panels. The bricks have a rich color nuance that runs from green to gray, with traces of coal burning on the surface. They are made in a thinner format than usual, thus enabling the consumption of raw materials and energy to be reduced during brick production. Rather than mimicking a traditional brick façade, the bricks are put in a standing, rotated bonding in the cast of the panels. By doing so, the façade gains a lively texture of vertical lines with the play of light and shadow upon them that would be hard to realize in traditional brickwork.

> "At first glance, the volume is modest, the layout symmetric, the object a simple cube. Nevertheless, the building does not come across as austere: The recess of the walls lends the body a playful character, the relief-like brick façade with its protruding windows gives the building a powerful impression."

The joints between the large panels render invisible in the vertical play of the façade. The horizontal joints are carefully positioned in line with the shifting orientation of the façade on the second floor and support the overall proportioning of the building.

By applying the pavilion typology and using all architectural means to scale down the building, the architect succeeds in fitting a relatively large project into the sensitive setting. In color and texture, the façade of the schoolhouse resonates with the play of light and shadow on the leaves and the barks of the surrounding trees. The refinement of the façade supports the architectural ambition and enhances the pavilion-like character of this fascinating extension that seeks to dissolve rather than contrast with its surroundings.

The two-story windows make the building appear smaller.

Framing elements with vertically laid bricks were mounted onto the façade.

KOEN VAN VELSEN ARCHITECTEN

Public Transport Terminal Breda

Koen van Velsen

PROJECT NAME
Public Transport Terminal Breda

ARCHITECT/S
Koen van Velsen Architecten, Hilversum / NL

BUILDING PURPOSE
Infrastructure / apartment housing

LOCATION
Breda, The Netherlands

CONSTRUCTION PERIOD
2012–2016

BRICK TYPE
Clay blocks
Facing bricks
Paving bricks

BRICK AWARD CATEGORY
Sharing public spaces

As in many European cities, the train station and the tracks in Breda have been a dividing line between sides of the city. Built just outside of the former ramparts, the station connects with a classical late 19th century neighborhood to the historic center in the south. To the north, factories and large social housing ensembles determine the urban landscape. The transformation of the station into an integrated public transport terminal has been the catalyst of a large urban renewal project to reconnect both sides of the city.

The new station designed by Koen van Velsen architecten is an impressive and well-organized combination of a high-speed train terminal, normal train terminal, a bus terminal, bicycle parking and a large car park on top of the station. In addition to the transport program, the complex provides extensive retail and office spaces and, most remarkably, 147 apartments. Two large, brick-paved public squares connect the complex to the immediate urban surroundings on both sides.

Brick is the main facing material on both the inside and outside walls, lending the monumental complex a scale we can physically relate to. The warm-colored, soft hand-molded bricks of the main façade surfaces are combined with a darker and hard wire cut brick in the plinth to deal with the intensive use of the spaces. Resonating with historic buildings where traces of alterations and extensions made over time are often visible in the brickwork, surfaces of differently colored bricks are applied on the façades. These surfaces are inspired by changes made in the design during the process, like the shifting of a window, and are executed in slightly contrasting, differently sized bricks and especially glazed bricks. These seemingly independent surfaces contribute to the scaling of the complex and provide a fascinating play over the façades that relativizes the rational organization of the terminal building, the offices and the housing behind.

> "Inspiration was drawn from historic Italian cities, in which brickwork façades express the changes over time."

The use of a single material ties not only all the different functions in this large complex together, it also creates a direct and recognizable link between the new complex and the existing brick buildings of various ages and ambitions on both sides of the station. Where many contemporary infrastructural buildings that end up in spectacular roofs spanning over rationally organized programs actually alienate and disengage with the urban surroundings, the Breda terminal provides a successful alternative. The complex is conceived first and foremost as a classical urban building, a recognizable type in the city. By adding conventional urban programs to its façade, it has an attractive face to both sides of the station. In addition, by using the same material most of the surroundings have been built up with, the transport terminal succeeds in its ultimate ambition in becoming the connection between the formerly separated parts of the city.

Sharing public spaces

The terminal connects the previously separated parts of the city.

Bricks establish the connection between the individual components of the traffic hub and the structures in the surroundings.

The pattern could be read as a reaction to changes during the implementation process.

Building outside the box

MIKKO SUMMANEN

From Clay to Gold – Innovative Concepts and Ways of Using Bricks

Mikko Summanen

Alvar Aalto's most creative years are often referred to as the "red brick period." He was a master in using brick in unforeseen ways, which resulted in organic and human, yet powerful architecture. Aalto took brick architecture into new frontiers with his experimentations with organic form giving, reliefs and customization of brick as well as ceramic tiles. These experiments are present in his most innovative red brick buildings. Already in 1948 Aalto designed a student dormitory at MIT, deliberately using second grade brick in order to create a rustic feeling. In the fifties he designed the Säynätsalo Town Hall, the Muuratsalo Experimental House and the House of Culture in Helsinki, which are all acknowledged as masterpieces of modern architecture.

Aalto once cited Frank Lloyd Wright during his lecture in Vienna in 1955: "The brick is an important instrument for us in the creation of form. I was once in Milwaukee with my old friend Frank Lloyd Wright, who was attending a conference there. He began: 'Ladies and gentlemen, do you know what a brick is? It is a worthless, ordinary little object that costs 11 cents, but it has one very special quality. Give me a brick and it will become worth its weight in gold.' That was perhaps the only time that I had heard in public, stated clearly and bluntly, what architecture really is. Architecture is about transforming a worthless stone into a nugget of gold." This metamorphosis from a simple basic unit of burnt clay into innovative contemporary architecture is as true now as it was in the fifties when Aalto and his contemporaries built their masterpieces.

To my mind this metaphor can be in interpreted in at least two different ways. The first one has to do with the brick's potential as a basic material unit. Even the most ordinary clay brick can be laid together and arranged in countless different compositions. Doing so, contemporary architects have proven the versatility of brick in their architecture and will continue to do so. Today, the customization of bricks and advances in new technologies are expanding this horizon for innovation. Through digitalization, customizing bricks even in small quantities will become more and more feasible in the future. Drones and robots will allow us more freedom in form giving. Algorithmic design will help us optimize the structure and usage of material. The forerunners in this field like Gramazio Kohler Architects have given us the first glimpses of this new horizon.

> "Architecture is about transforming a worthless stone into a nugget of gold."

The second way to interpret the metamorphosis Aalto and Wright spoke of has to do with time. Brick is one of the oldest building materials in history and yet it still is reborn again and again in new contexts and concepts. This heritage within the material itself is valuable to people also culturally and emotionally. The brightest architecture always contains elements of both heritage and future. Brick as a material can serve as a bridge there. In the projects published in this book there are several outstanding examples of this kind of approach, such as AleaOlea architects' Old Church of Vilanova de la Barca.

Today, more than ever, we must consider the need for creative thinking in a broadest possible sense. Innovation and creativity must include social responsibility in addition to new forms and textures. In contemporary buildings sustainability and energy efficiency are often associated with the concept of "smart buildings." To meet the criteria for smart buildings they are, in many cases, solved with complex technology such as elaborate HVAC systems or multilayered building envelopes. In this respect we could call them "high tech smart buildings." However, there is another approach which is quite the opposite. Massive, homogeneous structures such as solid brick or clay block walls or solid Cross Laminated Timber or log wall solutions possess potential for becoming "low tech smart buildings." The positive aspects in these solutions lay in their simplicity. Too often we are facing problems with technical systems or complex structures which are too difficult to operate or maintain. There are also challenges in legislation, norms and ways of assessment for energy efficiency which, in many cases, disregard the ability of solid wall structures to store heating and cooling energy. These methods of assessment do not reveal the true performance of homogeneous envelopes and should thus be expanded and further developed.

Another challenge has to do with life cycle of buildings. It really is not sustainable to build buildings for a life span of thirty or fifty years when the other option is to build with simple, solid structural and material solutions for a life span of one hundred years. This long life span requires success in many fields, but by reducing the amount of complexity and vulnerable technology the probability for a long life is increased.

> "These awarded examples of contemporary architecture testify to the vitality and relevance of brick as a contemporary material."

Looking at the best of contemporary architecture, it is noteworthy that four out of six finalists of the European Union's Mies van der Rohe Prize in 2017, which is inarguably the most prestigious architecture award in Europe, were brick buildings. One of the finalists, Lundgaard & Tranberg's Kannikegården Church Extension, is a masterpiece of archetypal architecture, which succeeds in being ancient and entirely new at the same time. The winner of the Mies van der Rohe Prize in 2011, David Chipperfield, used recycled brick in a delicate and contextual way in the Neues Museum in Berlin. These awarded examples of contemporary architecture testify to the vitality and relevance of brick as a contemporary material. The awarded and nominated projects in this *Brick 18* book are proof of this same vitality. In all these projects the metamorphosis from ordinary clay to timeless architecture is true—from clay to gold as Frank Lloyd Wright so well put it some sixty years ago.

U.D. URBAN DESIGN AB & GOTTLIEB PALUDAN ARCHITECTS

Värtan Bioenergy CHP Plant

Helena Glantz (U.D. Urban Design) und Michael Krarup (Gottlieb Paludan Architects)

PROJECT NAME
Värtan Bioenergy CHP Plant

ARCHITECT/S
U.D. Urban Design AB, Stockholm / SE & Gottlieb Paludan Architects, Copenhagen / DK

BUILDING PURPOSE
Infrastructure

LOCATION
Stockholm, Sweden

CONSTRUCTION PERIOD
2013–2016

BRICK TYPE
Ceramic façade panels

BRICK AWARD CATEGORY
Building outside the box

BRICK 18 Category Winner

The sites for energy production and public infrastructure were originally located on the periphery of our cities. Due to increasing urban expansion, these sites have become part of our daily urban environment. Usually considered as technical design assignments, the on-going transformation and extension of these crucial and often hard-to-move infrastructures have become an urbanistic and architectural question.

The Värtan power plant is a case at hand. Located near the port of Stockholm, this ensemble of buildings has become surrounded by roads and housing estates, offices and other industry, as well as recreational areas. Several monumental oak trees and a fauna path connection on the site had a profound impact on the extension of the plant, which includes the world's largest urban biofuelled cogeneration plant. The new plant is a very large piece of infrastructure that reaches underground to the harbor for its supply of biomass and makes a significant contribution to the reduction of the city's CO_2 footprint.

The overground part of the plant has been clad in a curved façade of vertical ceramic elements. The curved shape of the façade unites the various installations that make up the plant into a single gesture, while reducing its acoustic and visual impacts. Its dynamic form proudly expresses the building's civic function.

> "The custom-designed fins that make up the unique curving surface of the building provide a transparency that subtly reveals the activities within – since safe, reliable and environmentally responsible energy production is nothing to hide."

The inevitable future changes and extensions on the installation can be realized within the building envelope, thus maintaining the strong expression and presence of the building in this part of the city. The unity of the façade is established by a stacking of vertically placed ceramic elements. The horizontal steel profiles between the ceramic elements not only act as support construction of the façade, they also give the façade a sense of scale, not unlike the stacking of floors, to which we can physically relate.

The façade elements are made out of paired ceramic elements placed in a V-shape and on top of each other. The resulting expression connects the new plant to the characteristic brick buildings within the ensemble.
Above all, the new façade positions this piece of infrastructure as a contemporary building that fits within the tradition of the Northern European city.

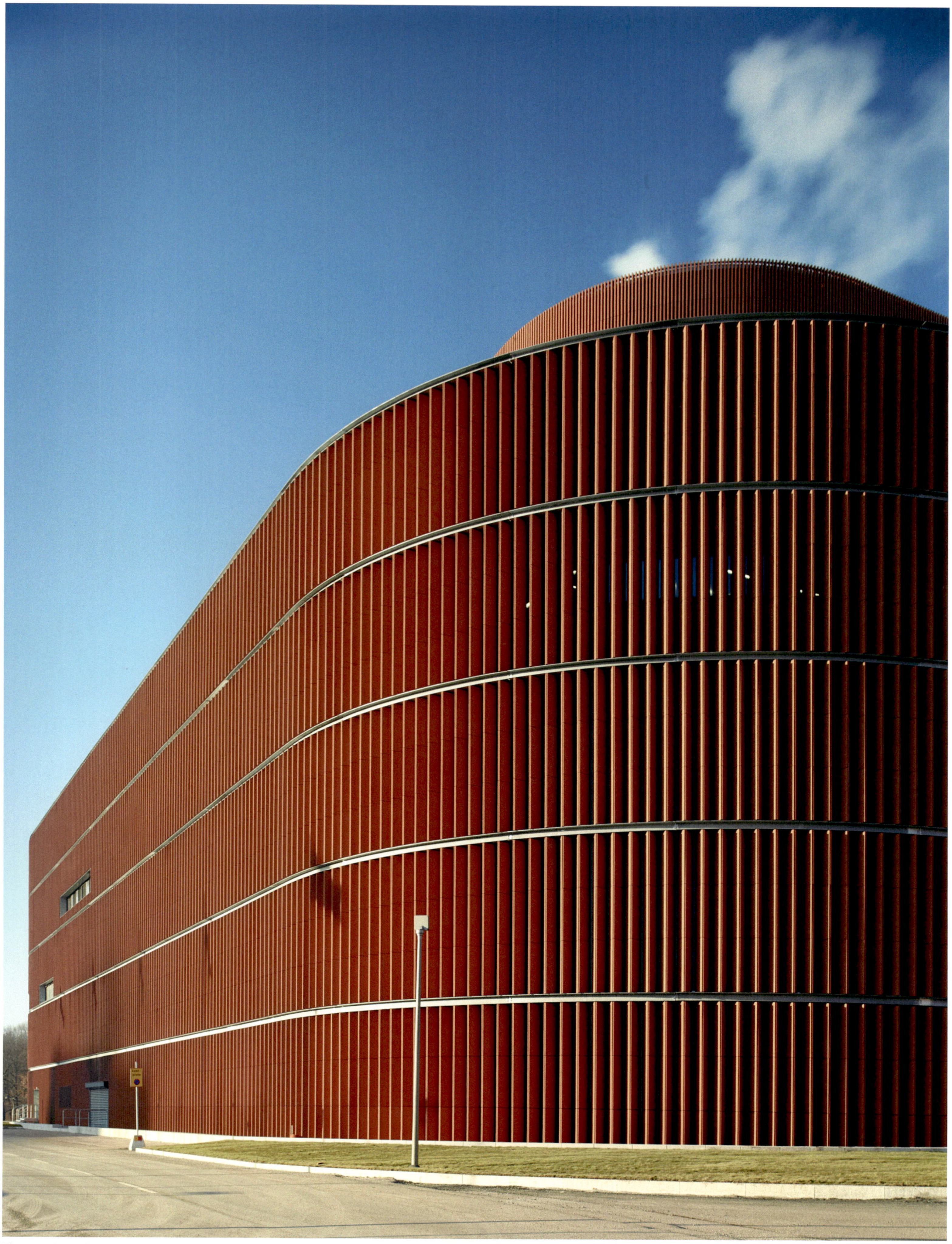
The envelope also serves as noise protection.

E4
E18
E20
HJORTHAGEN
Genie S-65

Jury Statement

"At the time when factories are moving outside the center of cities—it's a European protocol to move industry outside of the cities—this factory lies in the city with a great presence for tourists. The first example of a successful industry that becomes part of the city and doesn't have to run away and become part of the urban fabric. The texture of the exterior envelope and the variation of the bricks make it an attractive presence, instead of a just industrial drag industry—day and night. The building is very contemporary, but at the same time connects with the entire feeling of the neighborhood. A beautiful project which represents something that is unexpected of an industrial plant. Usually terracotta is associated with a more traditional, low-tech building, and it is unusual and innovative in associating the material with high-tech, industrial buildings. This combination is surprising and therefore very successful. It opens the roads for other industries to remain in the cities with new covers and with new, more sustainable procedures."

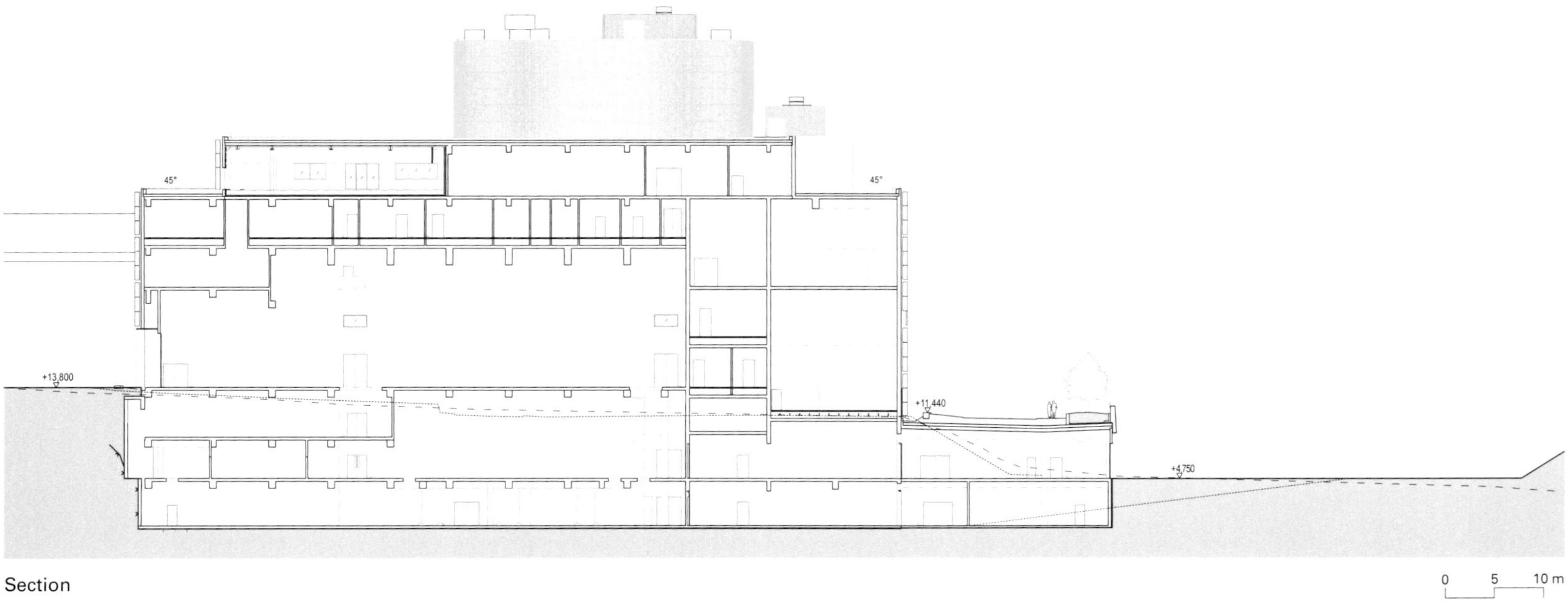

Section

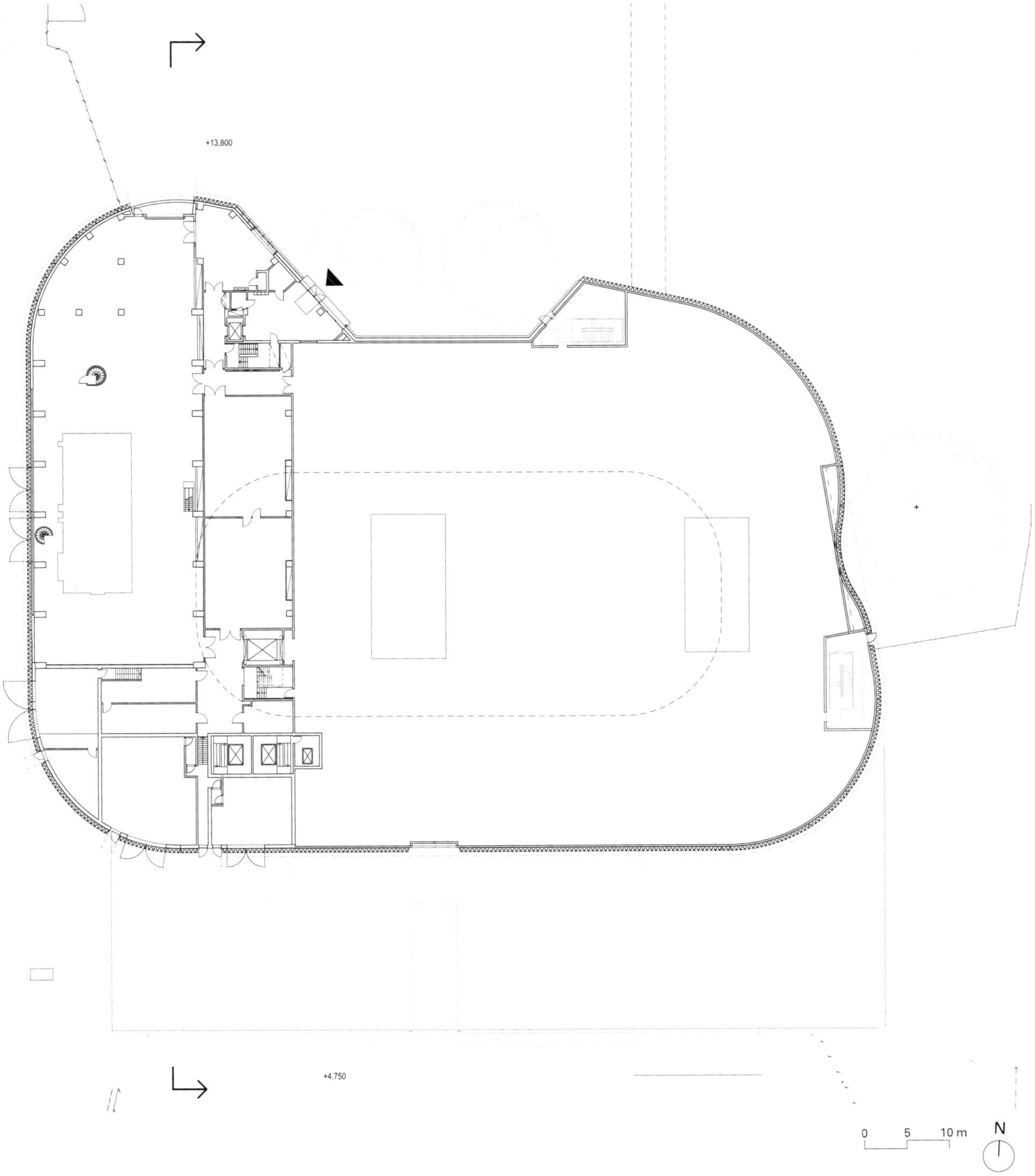

Ground floor

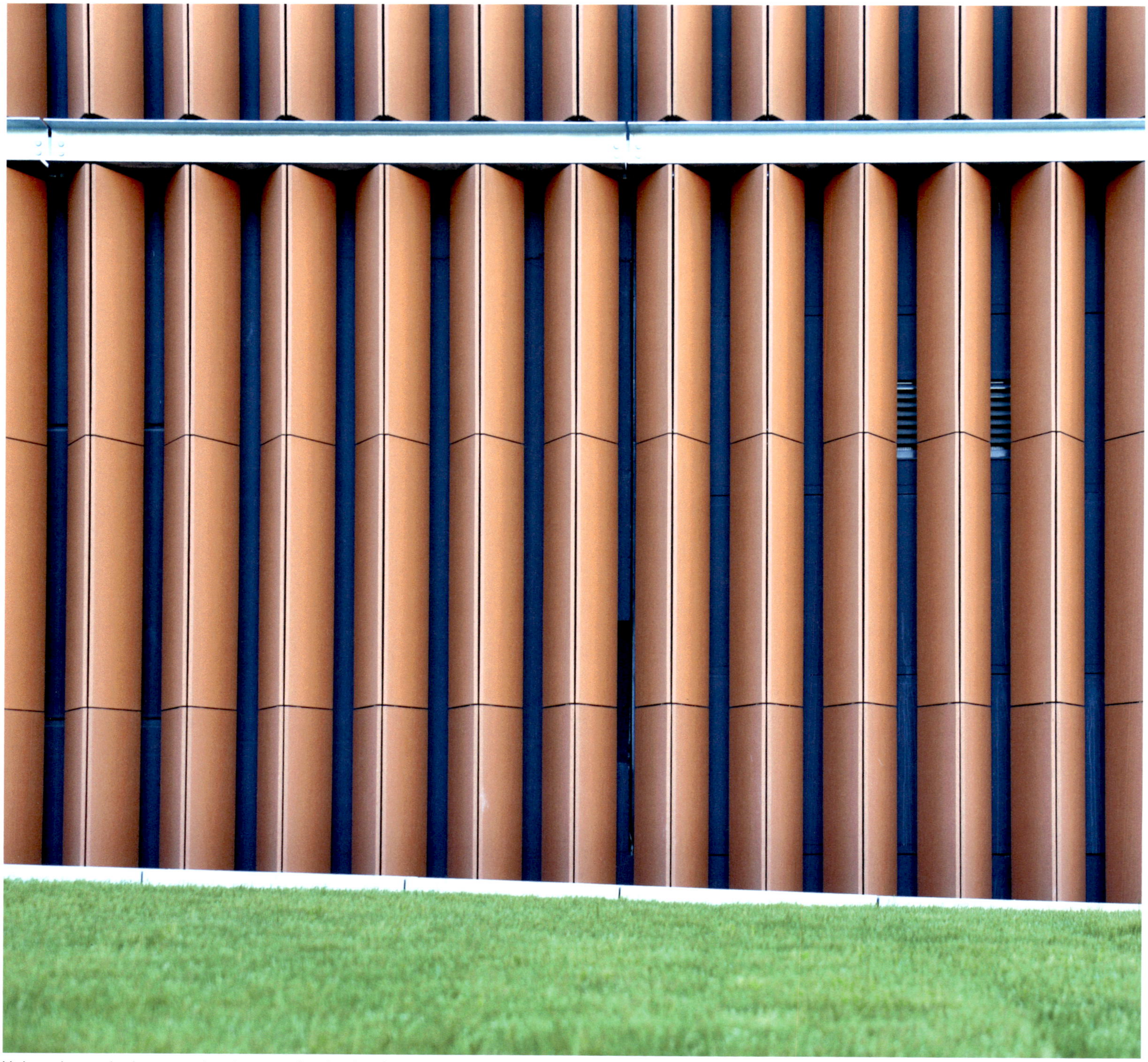

V-shaped ceramic elements, placed on top of each other, form the envelope for the entire plant.

The plant in the urban context

ALEAOLEA ARCHITECTURE & LANDSCAPE

The Old Church of Vilanova de la Barca

Roger Such, Laia Renalias, Nawl Laroui, Carles Serrano, Leticia Soriano

PROJECT NAME
The Old Church of Vilanova de la Barca

ARCHITECT/S
AleaOlea architecture & landscape, Barcelona / ES

BUILDING PURPOSE
Multipurpose hall

LOCATION
Lleida, Spain

CONSTRUCTION PERIOD
2015–2016

BRICK TYPE
Facing bricks
Roof tiles

BRICK AWARD CATEGORY
Building outside the box

BRICK 18 **Special Prize Winner**

"All architecture proposes an effect on the human mind," the British thinker and writer John Ruskin said some time ago, and "not merely a service for the human frame." The revitalization of the church of Vilanova de la Barca in the heart of Catalonia does both. It is not only a protective measure for ruinous wall remains that slumbered away for decades and had already nearly lost the battle against nature, but also a story that became a manifesto, making the stirring history of this site readable and experienceable for the first time.

Erected in the 13th century, the church is mainly Romanesque, but pointed arches and the apse make the Gothic influences noticeable. An abrupt breach took place in 1936: During the first months of the Spanish Civil War, the town of Vilanova de la Barca was extensively bombed. The destruction also did not spare the little church. For more than 80 years the walls lay waste.

In 2009, a decision was made to stop the decay and to conserve Santa María de la Barca in its current condition. The Barcelona-based office AleaOlea proposed to reproduce the original contour of the structure, to complete the space, and to make use of the former church as a multi-purpose hall for exhibitions and concerts in this way. The building material of brick plays a major role in this time puzzle.

> "The way we used the bricks is a quite conscious connection to the lively variety of the old, heavy ashlars."

"We renovated and secured the wall remains and placed a type of ceramic bowl over them," explains Carles Serrano, one of the five partners of the interdisciplinary collective AleaOlea. The new envelope consists of double-shelled brick masonry with a loosely offset, porous bond on the outer façade and a solidly bricked, but airy-seeming layer of hollow block bricks on the building's inside. Various brick structures in the surroundings provided inspiration for the masonry work.

"The way we used the bricks is a quite conscious connection to the lively variety of the old, heavy ashlars," Serrano explains. The voluble, exuberant history of this location appears to continue in the small-sized hole texture. Ornamental light and shadow images fall into the space through windows set at various heights. In order to underscore the contrast between the old and the new, the brickwork was painted white.
The contemporary intervention of the architect is intentionally subdued in a chromatically aware manner.

A gabled roof with steely rafters and purlins forms the upper closure. Naked light bulbs hang on white cables from the ceiling and lend the space a nearly workshop-like character. In the apse on the east side, the lamps are consolidated into a minimalistic chandelier. The space allocation plan is extended by a smartly integrated sanitary module, as well as a newly created entrance on the south side.

The revitalization of Santa María de la Barca is an unusual approach to dealing with historical building fabric. This project shows the versatility and adaptability of brick as a building material and creates a unique dialog between the present and history.

The view of the church was re-established outside; a hall for exhibitions and concerts arose on the inside.

An airy envelope made of bricks was placed over the remains of the wall.

Jury Statement

"The character of this building is established by the interplay of historic fragments and modern architecture. Accordingly, the roof and parts of the façade had to be newly built. Its missing walls are made by a very sensitive use of brick. The brick that is used is nearly white, which is not typical for Spain. Spanish architecture has a long tradition of beautiful brick stone, but this stone is not really in the tradition—it is not a colorful presence, it is more a sign of silence. The project is therefore reduced to its material and its substance, and not to its color.

It's a light, fresh, modern atmosphere designed by the architects using brick in an elegant, not simple-minded way. What results is an existing, innovative, but nonetheless traditional interpretation."

A gabled roof with an open soffit connects the old and the new.

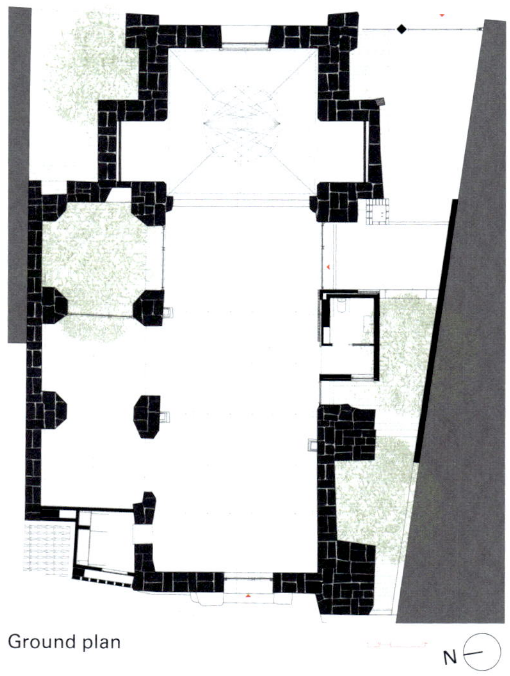

Ground plan

Through their white coloring, the new components take a backseat to the existing fabric.

ARCHITECTUUR MAKEN

De Gouverneur

Nina Aalbers and Ferry in't Veld

PROJECT NAME
De Gouverneur

ARCHITECT/S
architectuur MAKEN, Rotterdam / NL

BUILDING PURPOSE
Single family-housing / office

LOCATION
Rotterdam, The Netherlands

CONSTRUCTION PERIOD
2016

BRICK TYPE
Facing bricks

BRICK AWARD CATEGORY
Building outside the box

Traces of history, ranging from 19th century houses, open plots due to war damage and ambitious post-war planning and urban infill from later dates make up the urban tissue of the Gouvernestraat near the center of Rotterdam. In the middle of the street the architects constructed their own house. To secure daylight to the adjacent buildings and an existing small alley to the garden, the plot was limited to a footprint of 4.6 × 8.8 square meters. In order to keep with the prevailing building heights in the street, the house was constructed over four floors with a kitchen on the ground floor, followed by an office space, a living room and finally a bedroom on the top level. The architects aimed at a maximum flexibility in the use of the house. They achieved this through the positioning of the stairs, and the fact that the unique space of each floor can be split into multiple rooms.

This simple, yet elegant house conceals an ambitious story behind—or rather within—its brick façade. The building industry represents a considerable fraction of all waste produced in the Netherlands. Within their practice, the architects aim through design and building not only to limit the production of waste, but also to reduce the actual waste generated by the construction industry. In order to achieve their goals, the architects collaborated with the start-up firm StoneCycling in the production of the bricks applied in the façade of the house.

> "This new house in an old street complies with the old by the introduction of something new. Although the chosen bricks seem ordinary, they are waste-based. The waste is thereby the ornament in the façade and at the same time looks identifiable, showing the beauty of a circular building material."

The start-up has been pioneering in the production of building materials from waste since 2013, resulting in the series WasteBasedBricks. Materials used in these bricks range from waste glass to ceramics and bricks, resulting in a surprisingly rich palette of colors and textures. The façade of the house is the first project to be built with these WasteBasedBricks and resulted in a considerable reduction of waste by recycling materials into the production of the bricks.

From the outside, the recycled bricks do not differ from other bricks, but when cut they reveal their unique texture and color. The architects used these cut bricks in a decorative pattern over the façade, thereby adding to the overall appearance of the house. This building is thus the testimony of the guiding motto of this young practice, which is to pay attention to "the beauty of sustainability and the sustainability of beauty."

Recycled bricks made of demolition waste were used for the façade.

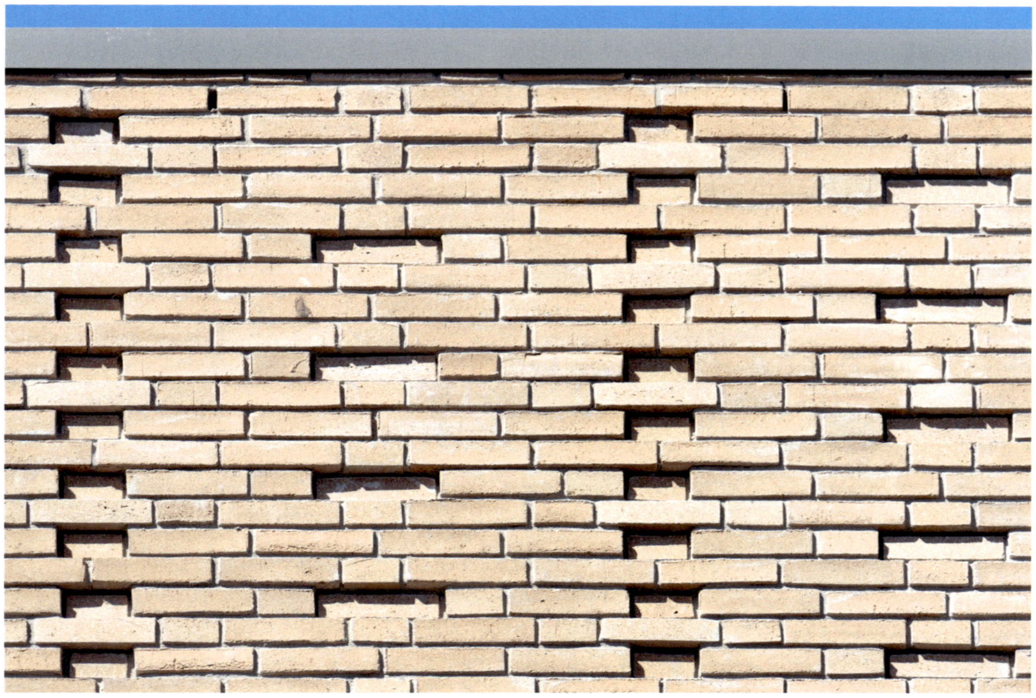

Cloaked in Bricks

Shobeir Mousavi, Amir Reza Fazel and Mehdi Kolahi

PROJECT NAME
Cloaked in Bricks

ARCHITECT/S
Admun Studio,
Teheran / IR

BUILDING PURPOSE
Apartment housing

LOCATION
Teheran, Iran

CONSTRUCTION PERIOD
2015

BRICK TYPE
Facing bricks

BRICK AWARD CATEGORY
Building outside the box

"Brick is a very popular building material in Iran," says Amir Reza Fazel, "but we lack a creative, refreshing dealing with it. After hardly any innovative brick structures were erected in the past years, this tradition has been disappearing more and more from the cityscape. And that is a great pity." Together with his partner Shobeir Mousavi, Fazel founded an architecture office in 2010 that has made a resolution to change this circumstance. The studio is specialized in linking tradition and innovation, as well as traditional and new construction materials with each other.

"And that is exactly what we have done in this project," Fazel believes. Admun Studio mounted a type of membrane made of classic bricks in front of an existing high-rise. These, however, are not cemented or laid in a mortar bed as otherwise customary, but rather form a light, airy veil by being modularly attached to a vertical frame. What's more, they are not mounted horizontally, but showcase their bearing side straight up towards the street.

The unusual pixel ornamentation was developed and calculated by means of an algorithm, which takes the spaces lying behind it, such as the living room, kitchen and balcony, into consideration. Depending on the light exposure need, the brick gills rotate sometimes more, sometimes less, out of the façade plane. "With the help of a separate software program we were able to structure the approximately 1,100-square-meter façade surface in a large-scale manner and to exactly calibrate the necessary light openings," explains Fazel, who even developed easy, unmistakable building instructions for the construction workers. "Despite complex design parameters, the brick mounting could thus be easily carried out on site."

The result is a thin skin that apparently pulsates to the beat of the city, not only making the house distinctive, but also offering the people living in it many technical and building-physical qualities that Teheran calls for: "Cloaked in Bricks" serves as shading, as suspended noise protection and not least as a thermal measure. A chimney effect arises through the air space between the building and the façade, allowing the warm air to escape upwards and passively cool the living spaces behind it.

"Especially important to us was also the function as a regulating interface between public and private space," the architect explains. "In traditional Iranian architecture the people live, introverted and withdrawn, around an inner courtyard. That is hardly possible still in such a fast-growing and densely built city. It is even more important to develop other adequate forms of privacy."

"Especially important to us was also the function as a regulating interface between public and private space."

Bricks were not only used on the vertical level, but also on the entire ground floor. The floor and ceiling of the foyer and the partially covered entrance area are completely "bricked in," giving the paths, steps and ramps a pleasant down-to-earthness and grounding the weightless façade one last time before it vanishes over the roofs like a swelled sail.

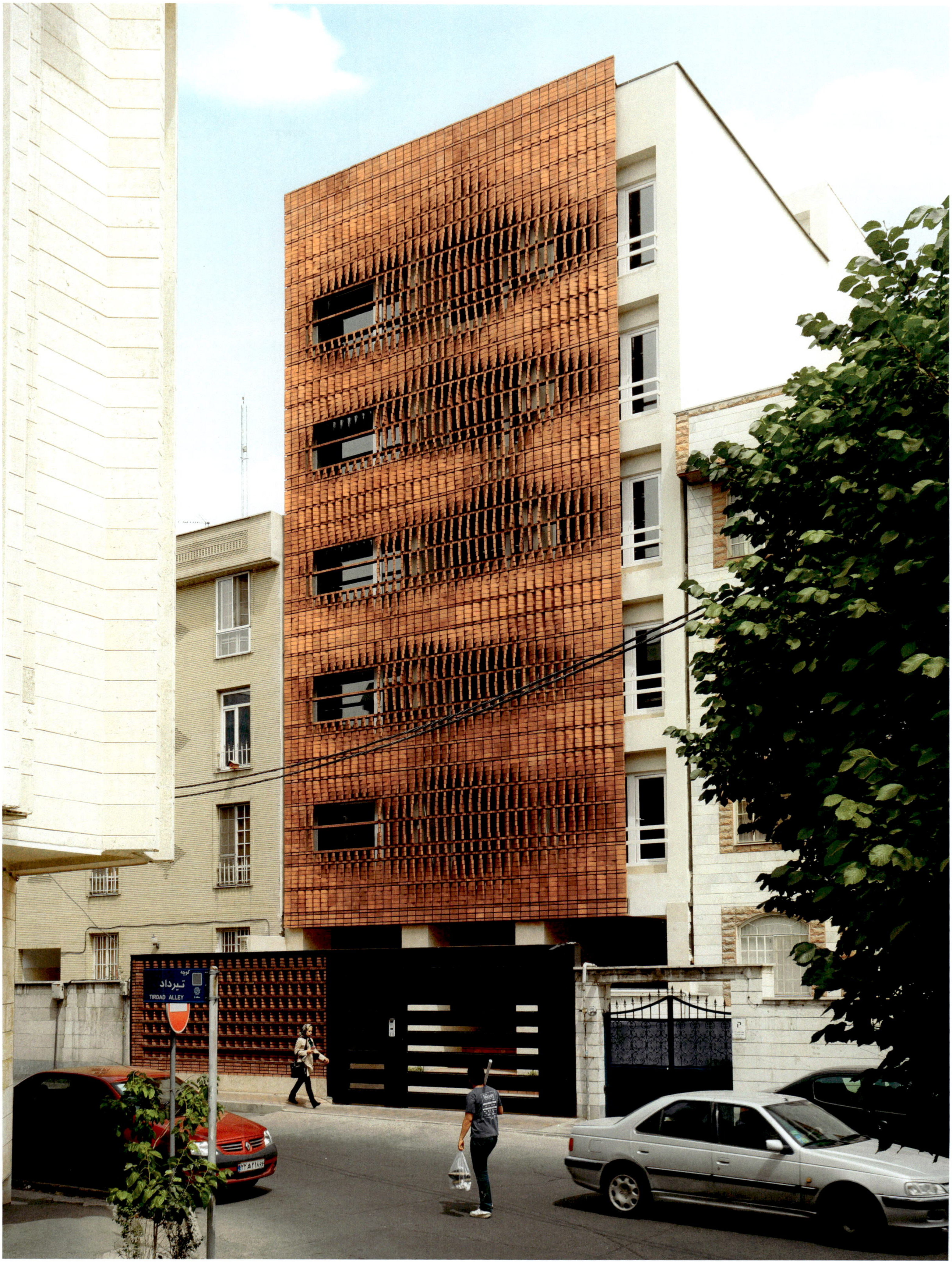
کوچه
تیرداد
TIRDAD ALLEY

The bricks are not walled up, but rather placed on rods.

Depending on the function behind it, the individual bricks rotate more or less strongly out of the façade plane.

MVRDV

Crystal Houses

Winy Maas, Nathalie de Vries and Jacob van Rijs

PROJECT NAME
Crystal Houses

ARCHITECT/S
MVRDV, Rotterdam, NL

BUILDING PURPOSE
Retail / apartment housing

LOCATION
Amsterdam, The Netherlands

CONSTRUCTION PERIOD
2014–2016

BRICK TYPE
Facing bricks
Glass bricks

BRICK AWARD CATEGORY
Building outside the box

Cinderella had her glass slippers to deck herself out with for the king's ball. Amsterdam now has its first glass house which dressed itself up for the world of high fashion. On Pieter Cornelisz Hooftstraat, only a few steps from the world-famous Rijksmuseum, the Dutch architects MVRDV erected the so-called Crystal Houses, a brick house based on the classical model, but with the sole difference being that large parts of the façade are not bricked with fired clay, but rather with glass.

"The global shopping streets look the same everywhere today," says Winy Maas, partner of MVRDV. One could hardly tell the difference between London, Paris and New York, between Prada, Dior and Louis Vuitton. "That's why we made it our goal to build a commercial structure that bears the typical local signature of Amsterdam from the top to the bottom and nonetheless allows transparent insights into the interior. It's as if the whole house had dissolved, as if it had transformed into glass with a single touch."

While a 620 m²-large business premises, used today as a Chanel flagship store, is situated on the two lower stories, the classically bricked second floor is reserved for residential purposes. Concealed behind the sophisticated façade interplay of glass and terracotta, which intertwines between the first and second stories like a three-dimensional puzzle, is a steel construction that transfers the primary loads of the building to the floor. Geothermal energy is used for heating and cooling. The depth probes reach up 170 meters into the earth.

> "This project proves that poetry exists."

"The architecture is one part," Maas points out, "but the really fascinating thing about this project is the years of research and development work that preceded the planning and construction." The basic research and the material research took place in collaboration with the Delft University of Technology, as well as with industrial partners. Glass bricks calculated and optimized in this manner were produced at an Italian manufacturing facility near Venice. A German company specializing in industrial adhesives, in turn, supplied the adhesive technology.

Glass blocks for the 120 m²-large and around 35 cm-thick façade were produced in three different sizes and laser-cut and polished. Dutch whole milk was used to check and guarantee the size tolerance of maximum 0.3 millimeters: the opaque texture and the high fat content made the optical examination easier. The adhesive, on the other hand, is a high-tech product originating from prosthetic dentistry and—like at a dentist's—is locally applied and hardened by ultraviolet light. Thanks to this procedure, the details of which are kept secret for safety reasons, the bonding surfaces can be dissolved and damaged glass bricks replaced at any time.

The Crystal Houses is a best-practice example of how technical innovation, material transparence and contemporary design approaches can be implemented in a historical city center. Possible symbioses for the future allow themselves to be derived from the unusual interaction between glass and clay which manifests itself in the façade. "This project proves that poetry exists," Winy Mass maintains. "And it provides proof that even the most tender and translucent dreams are realizable. That is the key to innovation for me."

CHANEL
ANNE FONTAINE

At the height of the first floor the glass bricks transition into fired bricks.

WIRTH ARCHITEKTEN

Remisenpavillon

Benjamin and Jan Wirth

PROJECT NAME
Remisenpavillon

ARCHITECT/S
Wirth Architekten, Bremen / DE

BUILDING PURPOSE
Pavilion

LOCATION
Affinghausen, Germany

CONSTRUCTION PERIOD
2014–2015

BRICK TYPE
Re-used bricks

BRICK AWARD CATEGORY
Building outside the box

A garage was needed—at the beginning. The pavilion that ultimately emerged can also serve as such. Two cars have space in it; thanks to the ceiling height of almost 2.5 meters, a small tractor could also be parked in it. Wood can be stored and processed here: A functional agricultural building, a brick shed located near Bremen, on the property of a farmstead ensemble typical of the region—it accomplishes everything one expects of it.

"The Remisenpavillon completes a typical old farm ensemble of the Lower Saxony region in Germany, continuing the existing building lines, the traditional scale and building materials."

Yet the architects made more out of this nondescript building assignment. What developed was a structure, consisting of bricks, concrete and an old oak tree, in which the idea of pavilions from the parks of aristocratic estates lives on somewhat, serving to provide shelter, to take something in, to withdraw to, but which likewise were an expression of educational awareness. The Affinghausen Remisenpavillon can also be used for dining at larger tables, for parties, as a retreat for concentrated working, or as a summer loggia. Situated at the edge of the lot, it is now the first building of the entire ensemble that is visible: a simple, closed cube, since it is accessed via the courtyard. A wooden gate on the long side opens towards the house; the two-winged gate opens across the entire width to the rear property.

Between a floor and a ceiling slab made of concrete, the walls of brick are undoubtedly something special. They are laid from the ceiling slab up to the upper edge of the roof and therefore on gaps, resulting in a hole pattern. The wall closes where the pillars supporting the roof stand; the parapet and base areas are also closed. In this way, the constructive setup can be subtly read. Towards the middle of the fields between the pillars, the openings become large, resulting in fluid transitions between the open and the closed. At the same time this ensures that the space is always well-ventilated. A wall support leads into a low wall with a fence that demarcates the premises and connects the pavilion with the main house.

Although the design vocabulary is modern, wood and brick are not only traditional materials, but actually old as well. The wood originated from a centuries-old oak tree that had been struck by lightning several years earlier and still stood on a nearby meadow. The bricks are likewise old—they come from a house that had burned down. The bricks were cleaned, but the traces of prior use are distinct. Old and hand-produced, several of them still display handprints.

The interplay of a utility building and an ornamental construction is also found in the detail. Inlets for the ceiling lamps are gilded, lending nobility to the simple light bulb fitting without seeming wrong or out of place. In this mixture of clear form and craftsmanship, the pavilion is a statement for the fact that the past and the present can be combined without loud gesturing.

The bricks originate from a burnt-out ruin, the wood from a dead oak tree.

The steel frames in the small loggia area can swivel around their central axes.

The ornamental-like structure of the façade is the result of bricks arranged vertically and edgewise, as well as rotated at a 90-degree angle.

Lanka Learning Center

feat.collective

PROJECT NAME
Lanka Learning Center

ARCHITECT/S
feat.collective,
Stuttgart / DE,
Zurich / CH,
Ahmedabad / IN

BUILDING PURPOSE
Education

LOCATION
Parangiyamadu,
Sri Lanka

CONSTRUCTION PERIOD
2015–2016

BRICK TYPE
Facing bricks

BRICK AWARD CATEGORY
Building outside the box

Parangiyamadu is a small fishing village to the south of Kalduday in Sri Lanka. The region has suffered largely from the ethnic civil war and the disastrous tsunami of 2004. Thus, the Lanka Learning Center was initiated with the goal of reconciliation between ethnic groups through equal access to education. feat.collective developed this project constructed with local entrepreneurs, craftsmen and workers after making a comprehensive analysis about local construction principles, cultural peculiarities and climatic demands.

> "Through constant discourse with craftsmen, we were able to acquire classic materials with added value in terms of architectural expression and climatic effects."

The center is located in a village composed of a randomly arranged number of houses connected by a network of paths between palm trees. A few clusters of vegetation mark the landscape and outside the monsoon period the climate is hot and dry. In order to keep the existing sparse vegetation, the center was placed with great care between the existing trees. The program for the center was developed in close collaboration with the villagers and consists of five buildings hosting an administration, a schoolroom for girls and one for boys, a kitchen and canteen, as well as workshop room. A water tower and separate entrance to the center are incorporated into the ensemble.

The center plays upon the archetypical community type with the building organized around a central clearing, which works as an outdoor multipurpose space. When entering the structure, one arrives into the central court from which the buildings are accessible.
A continuous outside wall separates the in- and outside, thereby lending the center a sense of the protected space its wants to be. Local construction methods were employed to build the Learning Center. A simple concrete frame of posts and beams carries the steel cantilevering roofs of the buildings. While on the side of the court the frames of the buildings are filled with wooden panels, all other parts of the frame are filled with brickwork. Depending on the use, parts of the brick wall are executed in an open bonding to allow the wind to pass through and ensure maximum ventilation while keeping the robust protection of the center.

An important part of the project was the actual construction of the center itself. Applying low tech and local building techniques with locally produced bricks and on-site cast concrete allowed the users of the center to get involved in the construction. It also ensures long-term sustainability, since all future adaptations and repairs can be done without help.
In this way, the actual construction and the maintenance become part of the educational goal of the project by offering young people the opportunity to develop skills. It also raised the commitment of the community members to the project. Rather than a "gift," the center becomes the own achievement of the villagers, securing the new center into the future community life.

Ground plan

The bricks were produced on-site; the house was erected with the help of its users.

In order to guarantee good ventilation, large sections of the brick masonry were laid in an open bond.

VECTOR-I ARCHITECTS WITH DAAD ENGINEERS

Restaurant Southside New Market

Ben van der Meer

PROJECT NAME
Restaurant Southside New Market

ARCHITECT/S
verctor-i architects with Daad engineers, Groningen / NL

BUILDING PURPOSE
Restaurant

LOCATION
Groningen, The Netherlands

CONSTRUCTION PERIOD
2015–2017

BRICK TYPE
Facing bricks

BRICK AWARD CATEGORY
Building outside the box

Southside New Market is a new, two-story, brick-clad building in the historic center of Groningen. In 2014 it was designed by Vector-i Architects to create a big restaurant (interior design by Matteo Thun) with a rooftop terrace overlooking the city's skyline. Located on a 32-meter-deep L-shaped site, Southside New Market occupies a plot that runs between Poelestraat and the New Market, and is surrounded by historical buildings.

"The project is radical in its approach, as the entire façade is prefabricated, but it opens up to the conventional practice of combining traditional brickwork with prefabricated elements, avoiding the use of secondary concrete or steel support elements."

The smaller façade on Poelestraat and the wider façade on the New Market are made to fit within the historic parceling of narrow houses along the streets and follow the overall classical arrangement with a plinth, a slightly higher first floor and a top floor. Over a depth of 30 centimeters, both façades develop a remarkably expressive detailing in the brickwork. Bricks are applied in a variety of stack bond and soldier course with special-sized bricks. Along the chamfered window reveals the bricks are placed vertically. Though the brickwork displays a certain tectonic integrity, it is—on closer inspection—clear that this expressive and complex brickwork was impossible to make on site in the prevailing North European building practice.

In order to construct the façade, the architects closely collaborated with a company specialized in brick prefabrication and applied a revolutionary technique. The entire façade of the project is built out of prefabricated brick elements up to three meters large that are fitted together on site and mounted against the main construction of the building. The bricks are glued together off-site by using reinforced glue instead of traditional mortar. This allows the brickwork to take up tractive forces and the elements to be lifted and transported. In themselves, these glued joints are common practice, but they normally result in thin 3 mm joints. Larger expansion joints between the elements would have been directly visible, destroying the search for unity in the expression of the façade.

This problem of the visible expansion joints was resolved by applying small ceramic strips between the bricks. Instead of directly gluing one brick to the next, each brick is glued to these recessed ceramic strips in between, resulting in a traditional joint width of 10 mm. This allows for traditional on-site pointing afterwards. The expansion joints follow the same width and finish as the normal joints, and are therefore invisible in the final result. Since the elements are prefabricated and can be lifted, they can be constructed in any position, for example, on their side or in a horizontal position. This enables the execution of these complex elements with a rich variety of brick bonding. The project is radical in its approach, as the entire façade is prefabricated, but it opens up to the conventional practice of combining traditional brickwork with prefabricated elements, avoiding the use of secondary concrete or steel support elements.

VAPIANO
PASTA | PIZZA | BAR
VAPIANO

The entire façade is built out of prefabricated brick elements.

Site plan

The design of the façade is related to the historic parceling.

PÉRIPHÉRIQUES ARCHITECTES

Lorraine Coallia – Paris 75019

Emanuelle Marin and David Trottin (Marin+Trottin Architectes) and Anne-Françoise Jumeau (Jumeau Architectes)

PROJECT NAME
Lorraine Coallia – Paris 75019

ARCHITECT/S
Périphériques Architectes, Paris / FR

BUILDING PURPOSE
Social housing / restaurant

LOCATION
Paris, France

CONSTRUCTION PERIOD
2015–2017

BRICK TYPE
Ceramic façade panels

BRICK AWARD CATEGORY
Building outside the box

Rolled out over the bars, bistros and brasseries on Rue Petit are classical Parisian, dark red awnings. Yet suddenly, behind a classic garret house, a bright-blue-shimmering sculpture soars into the sky on one of the street corners. The entire range of changeable, untamed April weather is reflected in the wildly faceted, expressively folded cassettes: At times the façade shines brighter, at times darker, at times a wisp of gold and pink flashes through, at times the cheerful midday sun, at other times furious storm clouds appear to be mirrored therein.

> "We developed a brick that, on one hand, directs everybody's attention to it but, on the other hand, has such a varied effect that no impression whatsoever of repetition and systemization develops."

The Coallia Residence in the 19th arrondissement lies in a colorfully patched together neighborhood between Bassin de la Villette and Parc des Buttes-Chaumont. Two apartment buildings erected in 1979 once stood here. In the course of a restructuring and re-densification of the property, Coallia, a social housing contractor, decided to preserve and convert one of the houses, whereas the other was to be demolished and replaced by a new building. The result is an apartment building with 177 one-room flats for migrant workers and a non-profit restaurant. In order to visually tone down the heterogeneous ensemble of old and new, both building components received a unified façade.

"We wanted to completely dissolve the borders between the old and the new building," recalls Anne-Françoise Jumeau, architect at the Paris-based planning collective Périphériques Architectes. "Therefore, we developed a brick that, on one hand, directs everybody's attention to it but, on the other hand, has such a varied effect that no impression whatsoever of repetition and systemization develops." A square 45 × 45 cm-large 3D brick tile with a surface enameled in an iridescent shade of blue, respectively yellow, was selected. In order to enhance the vividness of the façade, three different reliefs with two, four or six folded partial areas respectively were used. The overall appearance is that of a wild and yet somehow tamed, comfortable pangolin.

Years of research and development work preceded the actual architectural project. From 2013 to 2015, in collaboration with industrial partners, Périphériques first developed a digital model, then prototypes out of foam and plastic and, finally, the first workpieces made of stoneware and fired clay. The optimization of the shining enamel surface, which had to be executed to be resistant to rain, acid and ultraviolet light, took several months as well.

While the front, south-facing side of the building is kept in blue shades, the north side along Rue de Lorraine appears as a pixeled rendezvous of sand and sky hues. The color play is accentuated by tiled carpet ornaments on the ground floor. The laundry room, offices and meeting spaces branch off from here. Likewise operated by Coallia, the restaurant is located on Rue de Crimée. "It was a very intensive project," Anne-Françoise Jumeau remembers. "And it is a piece of architecture that combines the aspects of research, technology, craftsmanship, art and social responsibility under one roof."

The existing building and new structure were consolidated with a unified façade.

Three different 45 × 45 cm 3D-tiles are the basic elements of the façade.

The façades with the gleaming enamel surfaces are rain-, acid- and UV-resistant.

CIVIC ARCHITECTS AND BRIGHT (THE CLOUD COLLECTIVE)

Augmented Brickwork – Public Railway Passage Tilburg

Ingrid van der Heijden, Ian Lebbink, Gert Kwekkeboom, Rick ten Doeschate

PROJECT NAME
Augmented Brickwork – Public Railway Passage Tilburg

ARCHITECT/S
Civic Architects and Bright (The Cloud Collective), Amsterdam / NL

BUILDING PURPOSE
Infrastructure

LOCATION
Tilburg, The Netherlands

CONSTRUCTION PERIOD
2014–2016

BRICK TYPE
Glass bricks

BRICK AWARD CATEGORY
Building outside the box

The Spoorzone in Tilburg is the redevelopment of an old railway yard into a mixed-use urban quarter that incorporates many of the existing and monumental brick buildings on the site. The Willem II passage is a newly created public space for cyclists and pedestrians connecting the center of city with this new and vibrant extension. For the passage the architects designed a sequence of spaces. It runs through the existing tunnel under the train tracks and through the former railway workshop building. On the sides it links to a restaurant, a public terrace and several gardens. Hence, the passage is not only used as space for traffic flow, but also for cultural events.

"The materials, rhythm and composition of the passage refer to the classical brick architecture of Willem II Straat – in a contemporary manner."

The walls of the tunnel are employed by the architects to organize the space. While these spaces are usually redundant and socially uncomfortable, the innovative use of glass bricks lends the passage a surprisingly active and attractive character. Placed upon a robust plinth, a series of wall segments built out of smooth and curved glass bricks provides the wall with an overall rhythm that breaks the length of the tunnel.

"The wall structure inspires and directs the light effects and vice versa, during the day and night."

Although technically spoken the "bricks" in this wall are remote from the traditional understanding of ceramic or glass bricks, the "brick thinking" has been a guiding principle in the design. Based upon the measurement of the prevailing bricks applied in the old buildings on the site, the architects developed a new type of glass brick in close collaboration with the manufacturers. Thick, fairly rough glass plates are first produced and afterwards "bended" to their characteristic round shape. The plates are then cut to size and mounted into steel frames that form the segments of the tunnel. These bricks play upon the image of decorated, expressionist brick façades, as we know them from history. Each of the segments obtains a unique character by using two different heights in the 30,000 hand-made bricks and occasionally re-directing a row of bricks in the opposite direction.

In the daytime the light from the ends of the tunnel and the openings between the tracks is reflected on the walls and emphasizes the rich texture of the wall. In the evenings and at night a multi-colored LED light behind every brick in this wall lights up. The underpass transforms into an intriguing and endless play of light by responding to the atmospheric variations, movement and social dynamics in the tunnel. Occasional colorful associations such as orange on King's Day or pink on Gay Pride Days can be "directed." By employing all the possibilities that this "glass brick" thinking offers, the passage reaches far beyond an infrastructural connection and has become an existing urban space in its own right.

During the day the glass bricks reflect light into the passageway, at night they colorfully glow.

The Authors

SANDY ATTIA, born in Cairo in 1974, is an architect and, together with Matteo Scagnol, co-founder of MoDus Architects located in Italy. She received a Master of Architecture degree from the Graduate School of Design at Harvard University in 2000 and was nominated for the 2013 arcVision Prize in recognition of her exceptional contribution to the field of architecture. Her latest, co-authored book *Designing Schools* was short-listed for the 2015 National Research Award and her cross-disciplinary work in educational environments continues with her involvement with the Agnelli Foundation in Turin. Sandy Attia was a visiting critic at the Princeton School of Architecture in 2017 and at the University of Trento from 2015 to 2017, and was the Muschenheim Fellow and Lecturer in Architecture at the University of Michigan from 2002 to 2004.

PATRÍCIA BARBAS, born in Luanda, Angola in 1971, graduated with an architecture degree from the Faculty of Architecture at the Technical University of Lisbon. She collaborated with Aires Mateus, Gonçalo Byrne, and João Pedro Falcão de Campos and was project coordinator for Promontório Arquitectos in Salvador da Bahia, Brazil during 2005 and 2006, guest Professor at Carleton University, Ottawa between 2013 and 2016, and jury member of the FAD Awards 2016. Patrícia Barbas, together with Diogo Seixas Lopes, founded Barbas Lopes Arquitectos in 2006. Their realized projects or those under development include public and private buildings, single-family housing, exhibition designs, and interiors. The practice is also engaged in collaborations with architects such as Peter Märkli and Gonçalo Byrne. Their work was nominated for the Icon Awards 2012, Designs of the Year 2013, and the Mies van der Rohe Award 2013.

WOJCIECH CZAJA was born in 1978 in Ruda Śląska, Poland, studied architecture at the Vienna University of Technology and is working today as a freelance architecture journalist for newspapers, magazines and professional journals in German-speaking countries. Since 2005 he has been working at the Austrian daily newspaper *Der Standard*, where he is responsible for the topics of architecture, urban culture and real estate. He is a lecturer at the Vienna University of Applied Arts, as well as at the University of Art and Design Linz, and teaches communication for architects.

CHRISTIAN HOLL studied architecture in Aachen, Florence and Stuttgart. From 1997 to 2004 he was the editor of *db – deutsche bauzeitung*, and founded frei04 publizistik together with Ursula Baus and Claudia Siegele in 2004, where he published reports, commentaries and essays. He is a book author, works as a freelance editor, journalist and critic, and had teaching assignments in Darmstadt, Stuttgart, Wuppertal, Kaiserslautern and Frankfurt on Main. From 2005 to 2010 he was scientific assistant at the Urban Design Institute of the University of Stuttgart, from 2007 to 2013 editor of *german-architects.com*. Since 2008 he has been a curator and member of the exhibition committee of the "architekturgalerie am weißenhof," since 2010 managing director of the Association of German Architects Hesse (BDA Hessen), and since 2017 co-publisher of the Internet magazine *marlowes.de*.

MARCOS PARGA is an international, award-winning architect and designer, founder and principal at Estudio MAPAA, and has been a PhD architect since 2015 and Assistant Professor at the School of Architecture, Syracuse University, NY since 2017. Previously he was Associate Professor of Design at the School of Architecture, Polytechnic University of Madrid for nine years. He also has been a visiting critic and lecturer at various universities, works as a writer on architecture theory and criticism, and is the promoter and editor-in-chief of the annual academic and research journal *115Días*. He is currently conducting practice-based research and developing an educational strategy that both strive to recover the radical procedures of 50 years ago (which he explored in his dissertation), bringing new meaning and inserting them into a conversation about emerging architectural concerns.

WOLFGANG PAUSER studied philosophy, art history and law in Vienna and completed the postgraduate study of Museum and Exhibition Curator. He worked as an art critic, essayist and columnist at daily newspapers, including the *Neue Zürcher Zeitung* and *Die Zeit*. In addition to his involvement with fine arts, design and architecture, his interest in topics concerning everyday and consumer culture grew. In 1998 he received the Literature Prize for Essay Writing of the State of Lower Saxony. In 1999 and 2016 he taught architectural theory at the Vienna University of Technology. He is a conceptual designer, text writer, advises companies in developing cultural identities and is specialized in the cultural-scientific analysis of products, brands and markets.

MIKKO SUMMANEN, born in 1971, received a Master's degree from the Helsinki University of Technology in 1999 and did Master's studies at the Tokyo Institute of Technology from 1996 to 1997. He is the founding partner and CEO of K2S Architects Ltd., and an adjunct professor at the Aalto University School of Art, Design and Architecture, where he holds a shared professorship for building technology together with his partners Kimmo Lintula and Niko Sirola. The focus in his teaching and research is on innovative building materials and structures. K2S Architects are known for high-quality public buildings, innovative experimentation with building materials and forms, as well as the intelligent reuse and refurbishment of buildings. They have won several international and Finnish prizes and awards, including the Finnish Steel Prize 2016, Architizer A+ Award 2014 and Wienerberger Brick Award Special Prize for Hotel Paasitorni in 2014.

JAN PETER WINGENDER, Partner at Office Winhov, focuses his work on urban (residential) buildings and ensembles, the renovation and extension of heritage buildings, and on public and civic programs. He is involved with the office's projects in the Netherlands and Switzerland. Jan Peter studied at Eindhoven University of Technology and the Berlage Institute in Amsterdam. He regularly holds lectures, writes about architecture and is a member of various advisory and editorial committees and juries. He is frequently invited to be a guest lecturer and critic at architecture schools in the Netherlands and abroad. From 2003 to 2007 he was head of the architecture study program at the Amsterdam Academy of Architecture. Jan Peter has been a lecturer at the Amsterdam University of the Arts since 2010 and published the book *Brick. An Exacting Material* in 2016 as a result of his research project.

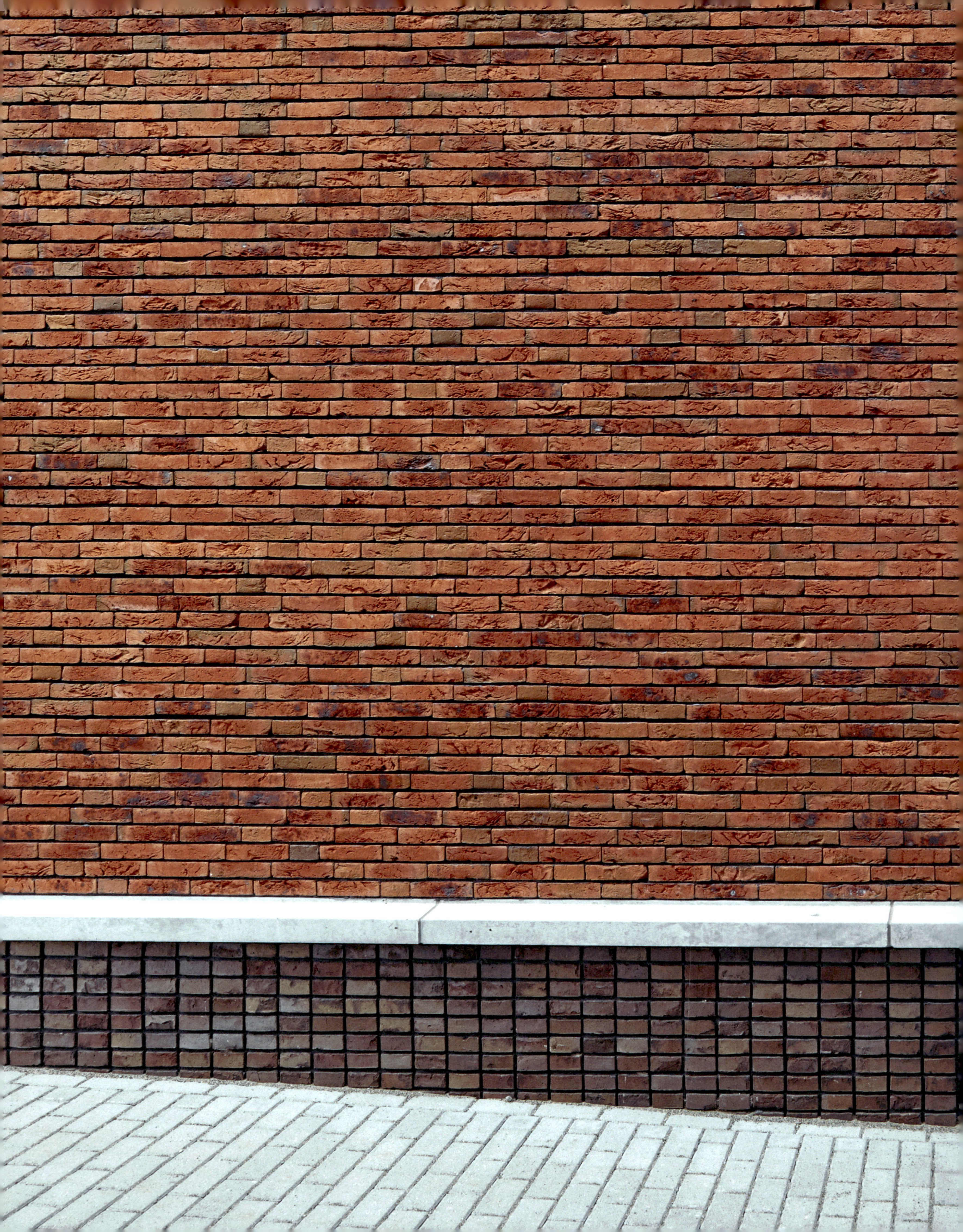